listening for growth

listening
for growth

what startups need the most
but hear the least

matty wishnow

LISTENING FOR GROWTH
What Startups Need the Most but Hear the Least

ISBN   HARDCOVER: 978-1-5445-3578-4
         PAPERBACK: 978-1-5445-3577-7
         EBOOK: 978-1-5445-3576-0

contents

introduction

You! Yes—*you*. You picked up this book. You were curious about what's inside. Curious enough to make it here, to the introduction. And that is in spite of the fact that the author is not famous and in spite of the fact that the cover of this book doesn't look like the cover of all those other books for startups—promising innovation, disruption, and transformation in gigantic fonts. You probably picked this book up for one reason: *you have a nagging feeling that something is amiss with how we think about growth.* That something is just not quite right. If this is, in fact, why you are here—welcome. You've come to the right place.

Now, whether you are an entrepreneur, a digital executive, or simply someone interested in startups, you're probably on board with the idea that being data-driven is a good thing. That it is essential for growth. And that growth correlates to success. Most of us have been living in that analytics-steeped, continuously optimized world for some time. Test and learn, hack the growth, tweak the algorithm, and repeat—these have been our mantras at least since Eric Ries introduced us to *The Lean Startup* in 2011. It's the Google way. The Amazon way. The "right" way.

We've immersed ourselves in the "analytics revolution" to such an extent that conventional wisdom accepts this approach as the best method for driving entrepreneurial growth. And why not? It seems reasonable that if we start with an idea, keep testing those hypotheses, and outhustle or out-charm the competition, we'll find our way to the unicorn's path.

But what if we're wrong?

Seriously—what if? What if I told you that path leads to nowhere? Or that it sometimes even leads backward? If our twenty-first century hacks, our algorithms, our analytics, and our Lean Canvases are so good, why don't they seem to, well, work?

Why isn't every entrepreneur living their best life? Why do so many founders and entrepreneurs burn out? Why isn't every product fitting its market? Why isn't every design a winner? Why is growth so hard to sustain? And why does it still, always, feel like such a grind? And perhaps most importantly, if the accepted tenets of startup success are so effective, why do most startups fail?

The reality is that even the smartest, most driven people in the world, using all the latest "tricks" and spending massive sums of money, make things that—most of the time—fail. And that's because what we imagine to be solutions are actually at the source of our problems.

According to a 2018 PwC study, CEO turnover rates had reached an all-time high while, according to a 2022 *Wall Street Journal* report, CMO tenure was at an all-time low. In 2021, HRMorning reported that 66 percent of managers suffer from burnout. The Small Business Administration estimates that the failure rate of startups in 2019 was around 90 percent. Around 20 percent fail in the first year, 30 percent in the second, 50 percent by year five, and 70 percent before a decade is out. And if you believe Quora, there are over one million tech startups born each year. That's a lot of failure.

And for those very few that do appear to succeed, it's fair to wonder: How many founders feel like their work has real, lasting value? How many created products or services that would endure into the future? How many sustained their financial performance *and* nourished their founder? I suspect that very few would respond in the affirmative. Companies like Loon, ScaleFactor, Munchery, Jawbone, and Rdio each took in over $100 million in funding and then, one day, not so long after they were born—*poof*—they were gone. There are hundreds more that took in less money, sold or merged, and then regressed into nothing. What kind of value is that?

I know the pain of seeing seemingly great ideas fail. I founded and exited three successful startups: Insound, Drillteam, and Clearhead. But I never ceased to wonder why all my big, bold, can't-fail ideas rarely turned out the way I'd hoped and planned. Throughout my career, I became more practiced and fluent in UX and product design, performance marketing, research and analytics. I like to believe that I also became a more empathetic leader and a more data-driven operator. I had every advantage at my disposal—software, resources, insights, teamwork, and ambition. So why did growth feel harder and harder? Why was the baseline always hyperactivity? Why was the steady state always unsteady? Why was I never testing and learning my way to happier, healthier growth?

I'm not saying it wasn't an exciting ride. There was never a dull moment, but even when I was flying high, failure was waiting around the corner. When you are winning, you just have more to lose. And in spite of doing what I thought were the "right" things every single day, my sense of friction and uncertainty only increased. How is it that I climbed this massive mountain, only to arrive at the top out of shape, dismissive of the view, and terrified of the trip back down?

Clearly, I needed a better way to chart the ascent.

Listening for Healthy Growth

The more I traced these struggles back, the more I realized that the solutions all came down to the same thing. And testing and learning or hacking our way through was not it. Software and algorithms were not the answers either. Instead, I came to see that there is one singular skill which, if deployed properly, could resolve all of these issues—for startups but also for any company interested in bigger, bolder, healthier growth. It's a skill everyone possesses to some degree, and yet it's also a skill that has atrophied in the face of increasing noise. It's a skill in dire need of resurrection.

That skill is listening.

Stick with me here. I know I might be sounding self helpy. But I assure you that this book is ultimately nothing if not practical. I also know it feels uncomfortable and illogical to begin, not with solutions or plans or ideas, but rather with the vagaries of "listening." But that is precisely where *healthy* growth is born. When we talk about growth we tend to talk about the top line and the gaudy metrics. Meanwhile, we obscure what's beneath the surface—the margins, the sustainability, and most significantly, the humans. Growth can seem binary—a trade-off between the top line and those aspects that offer lasting value. That's not the case with healthy growth. *Healthy growth is equitable. It is sustainable. And at its best, it nourishes the entrepreneur and the startup equally.* That kind of growth is rare—but completely possible.

You may be thinking that you already *have* experienced exceptional entrepreneurial growth, so you don't need a new approach at all. It's true that many startups can secure funding. Many can increase their sales. Some can be lauded as the "hot new thing." Some can even achieve frothy exits. But those are not the same as healthy growth. Rarely do those events yield more sustainable businesses or more fulfilled founders. To the contrary, they frequently end in regression or failure.

For over twenty-five years as a founder of startups, through the sprints and stumbles, I've become most convinced of this one thing: *healthy growth is achievable for any founder and at any organization, but only to the extent that we listen.* Period.

You can outwork, outthink, outhustle, and out-charm the competition, but if you don't listen, at some point either you or your startup will buckle. In order to grow healthy, we must truly hear what we desire as human founders, what our businesses fundamentally desire, and what problems stand in between those desires and the best possible outcomes.

None of this was apparent to me as a twenty-something entrepreneur living in New York in the 1990s. Most of it was still opaque in 2011 when I was in Austin, Texas, developing Clearhead. But through constant listening came revelations, growth, and ultimately, the development of a framework that worked in ways which no previous methodology had. It's a practice for growing better startups, products, and—yes—entrepreneurs. It's called "GPS."

Now, this all might sound lofty or overly simplistic. I hear you. But if you'll stay with me, I think you'll discover that GPS, while high-minded in spirit, is rigorous, pragmatic, and empirical in application. It's an eminently learnable and road-tested practice. A practice that engenders healthy growth—for any founder or leader at any company who is willing to listen.

Who Is This Book For?

This book is for founders and aspiring founders who are interested in the intersection of personal and institutional growth. It's for digital entrepreneurs with unmet aspirations. For people who are saying "One day I want to do this" but who don't know how to get there. Or "I keep doing the right thing, but it still feels impossible."

This book is for you if your own company is growing, but it's painful. You might be starting to feel the impact of the stress on your health and happiness. Maybe you're losing team members. Maybe the scale feels chaotic. Maybe you're wondering, "How did I get here? And what can I do about it?"

It's also for "intrapreneurs"—leaders within more traditional organizations—who want to harness the spirit of startup culture. These are executives who lead people in larger, venerable institutions—institutions no longer known for innovation. You have been asked to deliver oversized outcomes with outsized speed and risk. As with startups, you will not achieve sustained, healthy growth through charm, brains, or effort alone.

Perhaps you are interested in design, user experience, or product development that is accountable to both the user and the bottom line. You genuinely wonder what "good" work is—why certain initiatives lead to growth, whereas so much of what we do just seems like busy work. If that sounds familiar, this is also for you.

On the surface these two kinds of leaders—founders of startups and intrapreneurs—might seem distinct. It is, of course, true that a head of e-commerce or user experience does not define a company's mission or vision in the same way that a founder or CEO does. However, the mechanics of healthy growth are the same. The differences lie mostly in the limitations of power or influence. But a department can have a mission and vision in the same way an institution can. The same goes for goals. It's just that the further we travel from the founder or chief executive, the more we are beholden to others' desires.

That being said, even founders and CEOs are accountable to others—be it boards of directors or the markets. Rest assured that the principles we'll be practicing throughout this book fully and directly apply to any business scenario wherein the risks and rewards are oversized and the pressures of time and resources are highly constrained. Regardless of what kind of growth agent you might be, you have the agency to drive healthy growth.

It's a cliché to suggest that what got you here won't get you there, but it's true nonetheless. *If you want healthy growth for your organization, you're going to have to do things differently.* Rewiring is hard work. It's so much harder to lean back and listen than it is to close your ears and keep on running. Listening for uncomfortable truths can be a challenge. It can feel like a betrayal of your superpowers—your vision and your hustle.

I get it. I like validation as much as anyone. And who wants to face the disorienting malaise that occurs when you discover that "all the right things" you've been doing didn't bring the benefits you expected? Ultimately, I expect *you* do.

In the following pages, you will discover a playbook for healthy growth. Now, I imagine you've heard that promise before—a breakthrough system that will improve your business and your life. *Start with Why, The Hard Thing About Hard Things, Good to Great, Leading at the Speed of Growth, The Startup Owner's Manual, Rework,* etc.? Perhaps you've read some—or all—of those startup staples. I certainly did. And yet, here we are.

My hope is that in the coming pages you will get to know me as somebody who always wants to understand what separates ideas from winning ideas, design from good design, and terminal growth from healthy growth. As you read, you will discover the following:

1. What healthy growth looks like
2. What it means to "listen for growth"
3. How entrepreneurs can *hear* their truest desires
4. How to identify your problems most worth solving
5. How GPS leads to bold, measurable, sustainable growth

Obviously, there's so much more. You'll also discover a more intuitive and comprehensive approach to experimentation. How to avoid falling into the default hyperfunctioning, growth-hacking mode that leaves so many of us exhausted and stranded. And how to progress intentionally and empathetically to achieve the goals that are most profoundly true for you and your company.

These are the promises of GPS. On the one hand, they might not seem altogether foreign to you if you're familiar with Lean or evidence-based design or the Theory of Constraints. On the other hand, GPS assumes a significant overhaul of how you approach growth and success. It requires you to resist the urge to sprint ahead, toward ideas and solutions. It demands that you first lean back and listen to desires, goals, and problems. But to start, we have to address the assumptions you bring to the table about what growth is and how it actually works.

PART I

rethinking growth

chapter 1

Everything We Know About Growth is Wrong

I'm standing in a beautiful, newly renovated office in San Francisco. It's bursting with activity. There's youthful exuberance and innovation at every corner. The startup I am visiting is building an exciting new product. They're pioneering a new space. Their team is smart and fun and all in. They have the right investors, the right founder story, and a convincing thesis. They are racing toward unicorn status, growing and growing, burning more and more money.

Still, I had some nagging doubts. Their definition of growth made almost no sense to me. They had many direct competitors, including incumbents and fast followers. I was not convinced that the market was big enough to sustain the fervor. I didn't see any major expansion lanes. I wasn't even sure if they were a product or merely a feature. It seemed to me that the money and expectations were greater than the actual opportunity.

But on they went, growing faster and faster. Until one day, they didn't. There were whispers of an unexpectedly disappointing round. Less than a year later, they were sold for less than their most recent valuation and a fraction of a fraction of their desired exit. It's entirely possible that, within five years, they may not be a product or a feature. They may be nothing at all.

So, what was *that*? Was that growth? In this context, what does "growth" even mean?

In the 1990s, before I began my first startup, an online music retailer called Insound, I thought I knew what growth was. I'd never studied business or economics. I didn't have an MBA. But I thought everybody knew that the only way companies could grow was by demonstrating credible financial performance. You had to either generate sufficient profit margins to sustain future expansion or you had to provide evidence that your top line improvements or potential improvements were indicative of a future wherein profits were inevitable. In either scenario, growth was measured by profits and losses, prices and earnings. And the overall equity value of a company reflected those ratios. *A business that showed a predictable ascent, or at least a clear path to profitability—that was something worth investing in.*

I approached Insound with this basic premise in mind. I didn't start it with any notions of developing outsized wealth or creating a massive online, global brand. I loved music. Loved listening to it. Reading about it. Collecting it. And I wanted to create a resource for people who had shared musical tastes and interests. It was the 1990s, and the internet was changing the face of business, but I assumed that business growth still looked mostly the same.

When we approached potential investors, however, I realized that my perceptions were increasingly out of sync with the prevailing narrative. Incremental growth built on margins wasn't enough. Growth had to be huge, and it had to happen fast. Profits be damned. The consensus on Insound seemed to be that the audience I was after just wasn't big enough. We could show a cogent business thesis and a gap in the market. But if I couldn't promise a path to hundreds of millions of dollars, people weren't interested. A new definition of success was developing.

As I looked around, I began to see that the startup environment was replete with shortcuts and speed ramps to juice a company for massive growth. Need to demonstrate growth within a short window? There's a hack for that. Need to get your next round of capital at five times the valuation of your previous round? There are ways to hack that too. Acquire customers at any cost. Buy now and pay later. Roll up a bunch of failing companies to make something bigger (which was always better). What I thought was an equities market sure sounded highly derivative to me. Even that phrase— "growth hack." I always understood the word "hack" to imply something negative, possibly illegal. Something in between cheating and stealing. No longer.

Business growth seemed to increasingly be described in two ways: inching along an incredibly long runway of tiny increments (which was tantamount to a slow death) or shooting like a bullet train toward a valuation built on assumptions and potential (real growth). I was no longer seeing the middle ground I had always thought was the essence of business-building.

To be clear, I have nothing against great financial success. I'm an entrepreneur after all. But I have a bias toward healthy growth that correlates to actual, lasting value for both the institution *and* the entrepreneur. Sales come and go. Valuations are derivatives. Head count can sometimes correlate to financial loss. But sustained profits. Retained employees. Evangelical customers. Happy founders. In my mind, *those are hallmarks of true value.*

In the early 2000s, several years after having founded Insound, I noticed more and more tech startups which were valued at astonishing, almost unbelievable, sums. Early-stage companies could be valued at hundreds of millions of dollars before their products or services were in the market. I assumed that this trend was a hiccup that would soon correct itself. But it didn't. During the next decade we still had premarket juggernauts, but now they might be worth billions. And all too often, eighteen months later, these "unicorns" collapsed spectacularly, flatlining or regressing, if they ever made it to the starting line to begin with.

I was sure that there was a word for this—if one day you're worth millions and the next day you're not. And it wasn't "venture" or "growth." It was "speculation."

We're still chasing the highs of that first dot-com feeding frenzy. People think that growth has to be seismic—disruptive even. According to this thinking, growth doesn't have to be a long slog through projections and budgets. It doesn't have to be gradual— that is for restaurants or dry cleaners. Twenty-first-century growth should be a sprint around the fast track to a fortune and stardom. The status quo is to go big now and think about profitability later. That has become startup canon.

Unsurprisingly, similar thinking began to infect product and experience design. I first noticed it around 2010, during the dawn of the digital analytics revolution, when I started hearing about how to "game SEO" or how to "hack" digital ad spend. While I was trying to eke out a 2–3 percentage improvement on key metrics, I heard colleagues sharing A/B testing case studies that purported 25 percent increases in order conversion rates. Then 50. Then triple digits. At Insound, the numbers looked quite different. Much smaller, incremental gains could make our month. We'd test out home page images, search algorithms and new interface designs, all in search of modest, credible improvements.

Things only got more hyperbolic and illogical. The market became frothy with new optimization software and budgets for new departments. These costs are then justified with case studies that are either extreme outliers or resistant to the notion that most results regress to a mean. Little attention is paid to the details. I've even heard "test and learn" practitioners claim benefits that exceed the size of their entire business. While healthy growth is seen, heard, and felt, these claims sounded like "surreal growth."

And so, like startups themselves, digital design became gamified.

The hunt was on for massive "winners," and extraordinary losses were permitted along the way. In fact, they were encouraged. I have seen countless businesses ignore the opportunity costs and the actual costs of uninformed experimentation in pursuit of "testing everything." But oftentimes, when you keep testing and losing, *you do not end up with a pot of gold. You end up out of business.*

Yes, our prevailing definitions of growth are faulty. So it's no big surprise that we're misguided about how to achieve growth too. We frequently think it depends on a visionary startup founder with an outsized personality. On hacks and shortcuts. On hyperactivity and high IQs. On testing every (and any) hypothesis. It's become the collective wisdom for startups. And it's dead wrong.

Growth, to What End?

For every flashy "celebrity founder," there are thousands of entrepreneurs who started simply with a personal dream, whether an interest (music, sports, apparel, etc.), a skill set (engineering, design, management, etc.), or an idea. Every business begins from a kernel that is essentially personal. But that becomes obscured very quickly. When the fixation is on hyperbolic growth, the focus shifts from *Why do I want to do this?* to *What do I need to do?* And even before we've begun, the question of "why" is frequently set aside and forgotten.

I know, because I've been on this ride a few times myself.

I started fairly small at Insound, where my goals were simply to sell some records, provide a good service, keep the lights on, and make slightly more than enough money to live. Because Insound was such a thin margin business, I started another, more profitable company (Drillteam) just to keep everything afloat. My hypervigilance seemed to pay off because that company grew revenue and profits every year, from its start until I left. Eventually, we were able to sell both companies. With those sales, other people confirmed that we had created equity value. And that seemed like a win to me.

It was admittedly hard, however, to ignore the prevailing startup narrative. Incredible outcomes seemed to be the norm. Every article on Wired.com and every conversation I overheard in "Silicon Alley" seemed to suggest that 500 percent growth and billion-dollar valuations were the norm. Compared to those oversized outcomes, my businesses had merely *survived*; they had barely *grown* at all.

While I am certain that the prevailing definition of growth is failing us, I should also clarify: it's not all bad. The ideas of dreaming big and creating new products and services—these are valuable constructs. They drive innovation and, to a certain extent, progress. Entrepreneurship has a tendency to encourage hyperfunctioning and hyper-solutioning, which can, at times, lead to great results.

The costs, however, are extraordinarily high—not just for your company but yourself. I have pulled all-nighters and lived out of suitcases for my startups. I've had fifteen-meeting days and fifty-meeting weeks (yuck). I've been away from home for months of my children's formative years. It always felt like those sacrifices were necessary parts of the process. That is what entrepreneurs do. They take all those tricks they learned about good-to-great and product market fit and test and learn, and they work nonstop to hit those intense growth targets.

But all that sacrifice was made to chase an image that I never really related to. I don't like to work all day and night. I don't like conference calls or "dog and pony shows," or PowerPoint, or constant negotiations. I don't believe I'm alone in feeling this. In the world of startup founders, many are born introverts—they don't come naturally to the TED talk–giving, charismatic, extroverted style. I could play the part, but it was exhausting.

And yet, there I was, nearly a decade after launching Insound, poised to sell *two* companies that started with nothing and were now worth a whole lot. On the outside, and by most standards, it looked like incredible growth. I certainly felt massive pride and excitement. But on the inside, I was less convinced. My startups had grown, but would they continue to do so? Would they last? Had I grown alongside them? I was near the end, but I wondered if that end justified the means. Moreover, I wondered if anyone else felt the same way. I had followed all the right steps from angels to exit. But it wasn't until the end that I really began to wonder if I was truly charting my own path or if I was simply riding a conveyor belt.

What We're Missing

Why do we, whether we are entrepreneurs or digital leaders, continue to chase goals that we know are so obviously dysmorphic? Why do we presume that the ends justify the means when they rarely do? On some level, we recognize what's going on. As I write this, there are at least three television shows about antihero startup founders—one about Uber, one about WeWork, and one about Theranos. All of them seem inspired by the original tech antihero film, *The Social Network*. And all of them seem consumed with the massive personal carnage required to achieve growth by the standards I've laid out here. We write—and watch—these shows because we know how this story ends.

And yet, in our professional lives, we keep chasing. I get it; that path can be exciting. *But it's not sustainable. And it's seldom satisfying.* When you're laser-focused on marching down this particular path, it's easy to forget that it wasn't the only path open to you at the beginning of your journey. What would have happened if, instead of sprinting from "good to great" or from "zero to one" you had simply chosen to go in a different direction?

Each step we take in the name of hyperbolic growth moves us further away from a grounding in value creation and profitability. The longer we operate this way, the harder it gets to think about our wants and needs. And the further our companies get from our core wants and needs, the more danger looms for both. When companies receive investment or begin to experience growth, *the pressure to accelerate and expand inevitably disrupts the organization's nervous system.* Desperate for rapid growth, they move into anxious overdrive. They spin up new teams and projects. Silos form. Interests compete. Finishing a project becomes the same as goal achievement. Everything gets noisier. The culture becomes manic and loses the original beat as it becomes defined by a "more and faster are better" approach. Activity becomes aligned to speed and volume and dissociated from customer needs and benefits.

In the process, the core mission is forgotten. The founder's raison d'être gets rounded down to irrelevant. As you'll hear repeatedly throughout this book, this very same problem—the obscuring of desire, the misidentification of goals, the lack of root problem understanding, and the singular focus on MORE—plagues design as much as it does entrepreneurship. In both cases, *the pursuit of more tends to lead to what I call "terminal growth"*—outcomes that might appear like progress but are intrinsically fragile, caterwauling toward dissolution.

In other words, we all jump into the same funnel, only to realize when we come out the other end that we didn't get where we wanted to go. Or all too often, we don't realize it at all. The truth feels uncertain because the company or team remains maniacally focused on projects and initiatives even while they are unwittingly creating distance between work and value.

As projects divide teams and people are rewarded for derivative metrics rather than sustainable value, *everyone's sense of their own worth becomes detached from what their formative desires were.* Many of us assume that we can only solve this uneasiness by "leaning in" even more. We think if we keep outworking, outthinking, outsmarting, and outhustling everybody else, then we'll find success. But in those rare moments when we actually reach a successful conclusion—a new product launch, a great sales quarter, an increase in order conversion rates, the sale of the company—the painful truth remains: *success is not the same thing as value.*

In Pursuit of Healthy Growth

Years after I sold Insound and left the "music biz" behind, I wanted to start a business with a greater sense of purpose. I wanted to build a company that created *measurable value.* One where merit and evidence were valued over opinions and ego. Clearhead became that business. It was the perfect name for how I wanted my next startup to feel—clearheaded. Based on my increasing interest in the intersection of design and A/B testing, I saw an opportunity to reconceive digital experimentation not as something that you sometimes did *after* design was done, but rather as the very fabric of design thinking.

The few agencies that were providing A/B testing services in 2012 were more analytically minded than they were design thinkers. And, as somebody who was constantly being pitched by world-class design agencies in my former job, I never once heard from a provider who used statistical evidence as the basis for evaluating the success of their work. Meanwhile, the market was exploding with new A/B testing SaaS. Eventually, our Clearhead hypothesis proved valid. We grew and thrived and ultimately exited faster and better than I could have reasonably imagined. But along the way, I had to learn and relearn three very powerful lessons that changed the way I thought about growth and success.

chapter 2

Three Things Nobody Taught Me

From a relatively early age, most of us understand what it means to "have a job." We watch our parents head off to work every day. Eventually, we work for pay ourselves—we mow lawns, babysit, or wait tables. But very few of us have any sense for what it means to "work in an office" until we are dropped into one. School—even college, even graduate school—does very little to prepare us for the daily grind. It takes time to understand what the "TPS" in "TPS Reports" actually stands for. And why they are important. And who approved them. And why those people are in the position to do those things.

Similarly, no matter how many books we've read, there is no way to adequately prepare for the extreme highs and lows of the startup experience. The successes can feel ecstatic. The threat of failure can feel terrifying. And the constant effort to chase the former and avoid the latter can feel all-consuming. We can absorb all of the literature, but until we've practiced, we are woefully unprepared for startup growth and its inverse. I share this humbly, precisely on account of how little I understood about startup work at the outset. Years later,

I have the scars and the humiliations to show for it. As someone who has gone through these trials and seen the other side, I can tell you: there is a way to break the cycle and achieve growth that provides satisfaction and success for you and your company. And it can be practiced. In fact, it must be practiced.

If you're willing to hang in, *this book can function as an instruction manual for that practice.* Like any good instruction manual, we'll start with an overview of terms and key assumptions we are operating under. These are the basics, the foundational notions that set into motion my interest in healthy growth. And these foundational notions are built on three core truths. Nobody ever told me these truths. I wish they had, because learning (and relearning) them has been, at times, painful. But if I could go back to the 1990s and onboard younger "startup me," I would begin with three fundamental, if challenging, concepts:

(1) All that "stuff" we do at work—the products, services, projects, campaigns, and even those TPS Reports? Those are actually Experiments. We don't call them that, and we rarely test them properly or articulate the underlying hypotheses, but that's what they are.

(2) The most successful experiments are derived not from the most confident hypotheses but rather from the most profound understanding of the Problems most worth solving.

(3) All of those experiments, hypotheses, and problems are valuable to the extent that they nourish the core Desires of both the startup and its founder(s). And—yes—startups have Desires. And—yes—the founders' desires matter tremendously.

These epiphanies struck me like thunderbolts. And even if they don't feel quite so revolutionary to you—yet—I expect that you'll soon see the gap between what you know and how your startup actually operates. And it's time to fill that gap in.

Everything Is an Experiment

In most jobs, we do lots of *stuff*. We busy ourselves with projects, ideas, campaigns, and programs. We develop strategies. We design and build things. We hire, fire, and promote people. We get budgets approved. Five days a week (or more). Fifty-two weeks a year. Year after year. We call it "work." But *what we are actually doing in all of these cases is running experiments.*

Every new thing we try, every new change we make in business— as in life—is an experiment. Something new is being introduced and the outcome is uncertain. Make no mistake, every time we advance an idea—large or small—and see what happens, we're suggesting a hypothesis and conducting an experiment. The hypothesis may be poorly crafted. The experiment may be sloppily executed. We may never measure the results. We are unlikely to use the language of science. But that's what we are doing. I know, the terms sound like the stuff of high school chemistry. But they're useful to describe what we do every day.

If you've read *The Lean Startup* or if you've dabbled in digital optimization, this claim may not surprise you. But in 2001, it floored me. In fact, it probably saved my first startup from dissolution. Back then, at Insound, we designed and built a new feature for practically every idea we had. We were not alone in our reckless experimentation (a term we never used at the time). We launched our website at a moment when the push for innovation was extraordinary. The internet was new. As an online music store serving a technically precocious customer base, we felt compelled to keep up with the expectations of our users and the momentum of the new internet economy.

The possibilities were seemingly endless. And there were no real codified design or engineering patterns that had been tested and proven out. Every website was a snowflake—you could do horizontal navigation or vertical, put checkout on page one or page eight, etc. We designed and built the interface from scratch. At the same time, every idea we had seemed worth pursuing. Bring in bands for nightly "chats" with fans? Sure—let's do it! Stream indie music videos that hadn't been widely released to the public? We're on it! We'll even make our own media player! There's no off-the-shelf affiliate program? Minor obstacle. Let's get our designers and engineers to make that before month's end. Our process was simply this: idea, design, build, and release. Our philosophy was even simpler: more and faster.

We had started as a site where customers could buy indie rock records. Simple, right? But we just started churning new ideas out. We assumed that if we were the first to do it, we would get more traffic—which was all anybody seemed to care about at the time—and that said traffic would inevitably lead to more sales. And so, we redesigned the site, more than once, and in more than one way. Not surprisingly, our user experience and interface ended up a mish-mash nightmare to navigate—every feature and every page looked completely different. Customers had no idea where they were in the store, and when it came time to checkout, look out. We had not one, but two different checkout processes, depending on how the product was shipped. In truth, we hadn't designed the site at all; we'd "Frankensteined" it.

Intuitively, we knew it was not working. All of our novel ideas had led to a website that was hard to use, hard to support, and frankly, ugly. Worst of all, we didn't even have enough traffic or transactions to meaningfully gauge the impact of anything we had done.

Maybe we didn't need to tear it all down, but I recognized we at least needed to get down to the studs and renovate. So we took a deep breath and embarked on a full site redesign. It would cost us a major portion of the money we had in the bank, but the alternative—the status quo—was unthinkable. Plus, we had so many new ideas that we were convinced were better than the old ones. We told ourselves this time would be different. We'd be smarter. We'd work harder. We'd get it right.

Redesigning the site was fun. I had a passion for design, and I was the de facto copywriter. The team worked their tails off, pulling many late nights and weekends. This time, we had design and engineering experts on our side. We'd learned from our mistakes. Naturally, the team was so excited for the relaunch. We were sure it was going to make all the difference for our lovable, little startup.

Our big moment came that spring when we released the new Insound.com. We flicked the switch and held our breath. We hit refresh over and over. We waited for the spike in sales or the droves of emails. *But that moment never came.* Nobody outside of our office seemed to care all that much. It didn't feel like a launch. It felt like a letdown. Whatever we had done was apparently a wash—and that was gutting. All that work. All those ideas. All that brainpower. All that money! It was then I realized that our redesign was not a "project," "innovation," or "transformation." It was a big, expensive experiment. And one that clearly had not succeeded.

If it's true that misery loves company, though, we were in good company. Everyone else seemed to be in the same predicament. It was not uncommon for major, commercial websites to be fully reloaded annually simply because they were "stale" or because the competition had done so. Redesigns without proper experimentation were rampant, especially while the economy was strong. Companies would issue press releases about their redesigns, as though the investment in change for its own sake was laudatory. An entire industry of digital agencies was built on this idea without any type of performance measurement or testing. It was galling to me that so many bright people would invest so much money in so much change without considering the hypotheses behind the investment or the evidence required to validate those hypotheses.

Looking around, I realized that the current thinking was flawed—not just for Insound but for nearly every online startup out there. It was perhaps even worse for the incumbent, non-digital businesses that were trying to catch up to e-commerce. They were investing more and more on new web design, development, features, and products—effectively on running a bunch of experiments—without testing them. Even if they could afford to test, they rarely did. And in those extremely rare instances when they did, they could not test properly, because they had not even articulated clear, specific hypotheses to begin with.

In time, and in conjunction with the ascent of digital analytics and Lean thinking, my aperture widened. I recognized that it was not simply our digital initiatives that were caterwauling as untested experiments. It wasn't just the new designs and features and products and campaigns. It was the whole business. *Market-facing changes were eventually subject to testing and validation, but what about overhead and operations and administration?* The "GA" (general and administrative) on the financial statement? That was a big number. Weren't those changes also experiments?

I became inspired by this realization. Some might even say obsessed. Where before I saw ideas and projects, I could now only hear the unspoken hypotheses and experiments. And yet, as recently as 2010, nobody else seemed to be talking about it. It was driving me crazy. Ultimately, I started Clearhead to talk about it. And to do something about it. Back in 2012, Clearhead was founded as an agency devoted to gathering and validating those hypotheses.

To us, ideas were cheap. Everyone had opinions. Ideas lacked clarity, precision, and certainty. Hypotheses were ideas rendered naked of hubris. *They were ideas restated as specific claims of change, including their benefits and success metrics.* As an agency, we were obsessed with hypotheses. For several years, when I wondered where winning experiments (and ultimately healthy growth) came from, I was convinced that the answer was "great hypotheses." It turned out that I was not exactly right. But I was getting closer.

Some Problems are More Worth Solving than Others

After founding Clearhead, I spent most of my waking hours wondering what led to positive, confident outcomes for our clients and, of course, for my own startup. After all, we were in the business of optimization through experimentation. Our work was significantly enhanced and accelerated by the increased adoption of Lean Startup principles and a bevy of new, game-changing A/B testing software platforms. We were testing digital designs and features at an unprecedented pace and with equal exuberance. We thought, "Finally—we are doing it right!"

Well, almost. My co-founder at Clearhead was Ryan Garner. Ryan and I had worked together at Warner Music Group in the years after I'd sold Insound, and we made a great team. When we started Clearhead, we were excited about the possibilities for new experimentation software coinciding with unprecedented (and frequently wasteful) investments in digital design and development. Everyone was getting hip to "test and learn." Everyone was buying software. But nobody knew what to do with it. An entire market was looking for continuous optimization, but very few people really knew what that actually meant or how it could be achieved.

Clearhead stepped into these conversations as both a translator and a guide, leading the way forward. We created an agency that designed and built things using the most contemporary methods and applications in analytics and optimization. The response in the market was swift and affirmative. We provided the people, skills, and methodology to match the new software and the growing business need.

In short order, we were winning competitive bids against more traditional design firms because our pitch was simple: You could buy design from a hundred great agencies, but how many could show you whether it worked or didn't work? And why or why not? Well, we could. In fact, that's why we existed.

We got business from Dell, Patagonia, and Ralph Lauren all within the first few months. Companies wanted to buy our services, and we were able to help them test and learn rapidly. We were doing everything "right" according to the Lean Startup model. Our mantra was align, validate, optimize, and sustain. And in that model, every test was valuable; outcomes didn't matter as much as the learning that was taking place. *That assumption—that "fast failure" was admirable—seemed logical* and possibly desirable when compared to "slow failure." It was a hallmark of Lean. But as an entrepreneur obsessed with value creation and sensitive to the actual profits since before the Insound days, something about the opportunity cost of "failing into success" did not sit well. In those halcyon days when Clearhead was growing like crazy, though, I set the concerns aside.

At the time, I believed in our process. Our service delivery was designed around a Lean, virtuous cycle: Align around goals. Articulate hypotheses. Prioritize hypotheses. Experiment to validate those hypotheses. Employ research and statistical analysis to measure the benefits. Then depending on the outcome, either do the thing you wanted to do, pivot, or go back to the hypothesis drawing board. Both our clients and our team seemed to learn a lot from working this way. At its best, it cultivated measurable gains, increased learning, and provided more agile delivery.

But eventually, we made an alarming observation: *roughly the same percentage of hypotheses proved valid in 2013 as 2012.* We weren't actually "winning" at a greater rate. We weren't getting smarter or better at our trade. Or at least our hypotheses weren't any more valid. Further, many of the apparent winners ultimately regressed to a mean.

In order for us to be a great company—for us to grow on the basis of actual value—I knew we had to figure out why this was the case. Ryan and I began to ask ourselves the next, obvious question: where do winning hypotheses come from?

It turned out that the problem with our hypotheses was...the problem. This discovery reshaped the way we saw our world. The implication was simple: The more big problems you solve, the more value you create. The more problems you create or let fester, the more value recedes.

You've probably heard a quote that was wrongfully ascribed to Albert Einstein that goes something like this: "If I had an hour to solve a problem, I'd spend fifty-five minutes thinking about the problem and five minutes thinking about solutions." While the attribution is incorrect (Einstein never actually said it), the spirit is true. Lean Startup methodology, however, didn't really work this way. In the early depictions of Lean, hypotheses (not problems) were the magical sparks. But as we pulled at the thread of growth, we began to reconsider.

At the same time, we were noticing that Lean Startups were increasingly blind to the cost of failed experiments. You can't test everything. Not every experiment is equally valuable. Every business has constraints; time and resources are limited. If you try to test everything and keep losing, you're wasting time and resources. Similarly, if you make small gains on a tiny problem while another, larger one sits untended, that cannot be the best possible test of a hypothesis. It turns out that the key part of optimization is actually optimizing outcomes. Imagine that.

In pursuit of growth, we vowed to, first and foremost, identify and understand the root problems. Only then could we titrate our hypotheses and experiments to these elusive and valuable problems *most* worth solving. This revelation—*that while hypotheses may be the grist for experiments, problems are the fulcrum of growth*—changed everything for me, Ryan, and Clearhead. The germs of GPS functionally started here. It irrevocably altered how I thought about testing and optimization. And it led me deeper, to the next, logical question: *where do I find the problems most worth solving?*

We Don't Know What We Want

I asked myself that question—where do we find the problems most worth solving—every single day that I worked at Clearhead. But it was not until I left Accenture Interactive, the company that had acquired Clearhead, that I actually found the answer. It was 2019, and I should have felt great. I was free to do whatever I wanted. I had the means to try almost anything. Plus, I was genuinely proud of what we'd accomplished and how I had done my best to care for our employees *and* our value in the market, before, during, and after we were acquired. But then came the questions: What do I want to do now? What do I most desire? And was this the outcome I had hoped for all along?

I had no answer on the first two. And as for the third question, if the answer was yes, then why did I feel so lost?

I avoided facing that question for quite a while, but eventually, I had to dig into it. What did I, as an individual, want and need? On the one hand, I was successful at entrepreneurship. I was surprisingly good at sales and had developed a perspective about how to operate a successful startup. But was that reason to continue on? Did I desire the work? The cost and the benefits? Did I desire it above all else? In the back of my mind I knew I didn't. And I knew that I could not have clear goals for myself until I figured out what I did, in fact, most desire.

As I confronted this paradox of choice, I finally realized that I had spent the better part of a quarter century refining my own extroversion, salesmanship, ambition, relentlessness, and a bunch of other admirable qualities that came with great rewards but also at great cost. Specifically, I began to understand how and to what extent those skills were at odds with my innermost desires.

I had never taken the time to reflect deeply on that. But I had the time now. During those first months after Clearhead, I spent a ton of time with my wife and children, rededicating myself to my roles as partner and father. I took a series of trips around the country to meet with friends and colleagues to ask them why they do what they do. What did they most desire? And then, I dusted off some old Clearhead presentations I'd made and wondered if those balanced scorecards I'd designed for our clients might also help me answer a less institutional, more personal question: *what do I most desire?*

When I first asked myself that big question, I struggled to put words to the answers. And so, I asked myself again. And again. In as many ways as I could. What were my desires? Where were they? Why were they? I pointed the interrogation toward every dimension of my life. I kept asking those questions, digging through the superficial and the embarrassing, until I didn't have any more to say in response. What I was left with were my true desires.

Once I had rediscovered my desires, I wondered how I would know if I had achieved them. I realized there was only one way—by defining and measuring goals. *My* goals. That's when it all clicked! *Goals weren't manifested from a spreadsheet or from a scorecard or from thin air. They were inspired by desires.*

You see where I'm going here. By listening to my desires, I could plot my course toward healthy growth. Those desires demanded goals. Achieving goals meant digging into the problems. And through those problems most worth solving, I would discover clear hypotheses. And through those hypotheses, I could run the experiments in life that would most likely engender growth. By now, it should not surprise you that one of the experiments born from this process is the book you are reading today.

This personal revelation, of course, also applies to business. We don't usually talk about it this way. If you ask somebody what they want from their job, they normally begin with externally motivated answers like compensation or titles. But if you ask those same people what they most desire, you will likely get different responses—ones that are more closely related to personal development and growth.

The same applies for institutions, their operations, their products, and their designs. *Companies have desires.* Often, they are articulated through mission and vision statements. The more honestly and clearly those desires are stated—and then honored through their goals—the more likely a business is to grow. When you stray from those foundational desires—say, a SaaS business morphs into a services company, or a tried-and-true mid-market brand pushes too hard into the realm of luxury—look out! *Those core desires can quickly wither, and more often than not, the results suffer.* When we understand what they most desire to become, and when we address those desires, our work product is most likely to succeed.

Desires are so elemental as to seem beyond question. But I've found that in business, including startups, there's little discussion of them. Founders' desires are subsumed by external definitions of success and market wants and needs. Startups' mission and vision statements are rarely articulated as the loadstar for goals and objectives. They're more often conceived of as marketing exercises—copy for websites and employee manuals. And yet without asking and answering the questions of desire, how can we possibly orient our goals?

There are myriad reasons why we ignore this primary step. Inertia. Laziness. Confusion. Shame. Over time, as we become more entrained in our habits, more practiced in our role, and more mechanized in our thinking, we don't even go there. We don't ask the harder questions. We lose sight of that point of origination, which puts the destination at great risk. Not knowing the answers to these questions is uncomfortable. And it's tempting to jump into the next big thing rather than sit in that discomfort. Believe me, I know. But hang on, if you can. Don't jump just yet. Or pivot. Or accelerate.

Instead, I urge you to stop. Lean out. And listen.

chapter 3

Learning to Listen

Given that I am a man of a certain age who once ran an online record store, it will not surprise you that I buy and listen to vinyl records. I love LPs. I love holding them, taking the records out, and putting them on the platter. I like the minor clicks and scratches that arrive through wear. I love their scale—that they are one hundred and forty-four square inches in surface area where the compact disc is just twenty-five. I love the weight of their paper. I love listening to forty or fifty minutes of a musical arc, with a brief intermission to flip sides. I love all of it. But if I am being honest, I also struggle to just sit and listen to my records. I get distracted. I feel an urge to work while listening. Or to do busywork or Google some reference I hear in the music. I'm pretty sure I used to be good at active listening. Now, I'm not so sure.

I could say the same thing about podcasts. I subscribe to many and spend hours each week consuming new stories and information through my ears. But full disclosure, I'm almost always simultaneously distracting myself with something else. Frequently, I'm doing something on my computer or phone. Sometimes I'm writing. Sometimes I'm walking or running. Sometimes I'm ordering coffee (impolite, I know). Sometimes I'm responding to my wife and kids. The point is, even when I'm really listening, I'm not *really* listening.

I suspect that you can relate. It seems like our capacity to sit and just absorb what we hear without distracting ourselves has been diminished over time. The ways we sensorily engage with the world are vastly different now than they were just a few years ago.

For entrepreneurs and digital executives, the change has been perhaps even more marked, on account of the inordinate impact of speed and technology on startups and in the C-suite. In business today, listening is in short supply and high demand and is exponentially contested. So where does that leave us if my claim is that listening is the thing that most correlates to healthy growth?

What Is "Listening," Really?

Though my previous examples all relate to sound, when I use the word "listening," I am only partially referring to the dictionary definition of the word. When I say "listening" I am implying something closer to *the open and active consideration of information without bias.* It is an aptitude that requires observing and thinking as much as it does hearing.

Our ears are always open, even when our eyes or mouths are not. Our ears are the most constant, natural receptors we have. They don't blink. They don't scowl. They don't pucker. They just stay open to receive. Listening is about learning from our ears, but it's about more than hearing. As somebody who has suffered hearing loss, I recognize that you can listen without hearing in the traditional sense. *You can avail yourself of information—data, facts, stories, pictures, feedback, whatever—and then openly, earnestly consider what that information is telling you* with regards to a desired outcome, an experiment, a hypothesis, or a problem.

This conception of listening shares some correlation with curiosity, but the two are not the same. Curiosity is a social or physiological attribute while listening is an action or practice.

Similarly, listening is not the same thing as empathy. I value empathy in people as much as any other trait, but unadorned empathy assumes a bias toward sensitive projection. To listen requires a degree of sobriety, patience, and occasionally, dispassion for certain preconceived notions or ideas. Once we lean out and actively listen, I believe that we can then tune in and act with confidence. Sometimes, the next, best action is to empathize. But that isn't always the case.

In other words, *listening is being actively curious while being open to new evidence and perspective.* It is empathy-adjacent but not innately empathetic. And it is the single most important skill for an entrepreneur—or anyone interested in growth—to cultivate.

Listening for Bias

Today, businesses have more ways to listen than ever before. We have technology and software solutions for researching, testing, and analyzing the data involved in every decision. But does that mean we are actually listening better? Sadly, the opposite might be true. We are overwhelmed and paralyzed. We look for shortcuts. Instead of listening to evidence, we weaponize data to validate our biases. And in doing so, we're routinely missing the messages that would lead to healthy growth—personally, professionally, and institutionally. Listening is an opening up to questions and obstacles while resisting biases and unfounded conclusions. It is also about discernment and tuning and retuning based on feedback and evidence. To make sound decisions, we have to take in and carefully consider the feedback around us—even the feedback we're currently unaware of and the feedback we'd prefer to ignore. Especially that sort of feedback.

Put this way, the value of listening seems obvious. The question, then, is why, in spite of knowing the value of listening, we forgo it, shortchange it, or undervalue it. The answers are many and varied and, possibly, as important as listening itself.

Cognitive Closure

Listening seems simple. We are natural receivers. And yet, so many of us still struggle to listen effectively. This is partly down to evolution. *We listen selectively*, a human strategy that helps us move quickly away from uncertainty into the safety of resolution. We're nimble; we can react, respond, and make decisions on the spot. As a species, it has been to our advantage to recognize when we've seen a similar pattern before and to then jump to a conclusion. When you perceive a predator chasing you, your best bet is to run, and run now, even if you're wrong. But that drive for cognitive closure also impedes our ability to listen openly.

When we hear something that deviates from what we expect, we struggle. *We find discomfort when a narrative defies conclusion or takes too long to drive toward conclusion.* We feel a compulsion to alight on an answer, any answer, to resolve our natural discomfort with open-endedness, uncertainty, or confusion. Human beings hate discomfort. And discomfort in startups, when so much money is on the line and so little time is available, is perhaps the most acute form of professional anxiety.

But sometimes the drive for closure can make you miss something crucial. I was keenly reminded of this point years ago when a former Clearheader pointed out bias in our candidate interview process and compensation model. She believed that she was underpaid in relation to a male colleague for reasons unrelated to skills or merit. And while I heard her concerns and while they seemed thoughtful and valid, I mostly remember wanting to resolve the situation as quickly as possible. I experienced the feedback as a wound—and I did not want it to fester. So I sought out perspectives from other employees and colleagues. I investigated the claims, and concluded that she did, in fact, deserve the raise she was seeking.

She was just as capable and productive as her peer—perhaps more so. Our interviews and "skill tests," however, had been biased toward experience and public speaking. This particular teammate was still early in her career and less confident in her presentation, but she was also highly skilled, productive, and an excellent collaborator. It seemed cut and dry—we should adjust her comp immediately based on the new information I had. Further, we should also redesign our interview process to better balance skills and work product alongside experience and presentation. *Problems solved*, I thought.

Satisfied with the outcome and eager to move forward, I asked her if I could share highlights of our research and findings during a "town hall" meeting. I assured her that I would not share dollar amounts or name names. Though slightly ambivalent, she agreed. At the time, I assumed our entire team would want to hear, openly and honestly, from me about where we had misstepped and how we intended to rectify it. I assumed that was part of my role as CEO.— to own up to shortcomings in the business and to model openness to change. It did not take long, however, for me to figure out that I was wrong. After the presentation, I quickly realized that *my desire for cognitive closure had gotten in my way*. What I thought was transparency, many of my teammates considered oversharing. And given the power dynamic—me as CEO and she as new employee—my update and my apology rang hollow.

In retrospect, I get it. I wanted to move forward and move on swiftly. I wanted the discomfort of an unhappy team member to be behind me. And I absolutely did not want her frustration to spread. But my approach had the inverse effect. The employee in question and several other members of the team felt uncomfortable with what I'd done. I had taken the spotlight, as CEO, and rewritten the narrative to be about my problem-solving rather than the diagnosis and its implications. My retelling was perceived as disempowering and paternalistic. Moreover, I had proceeded so quickly and publicly, in part, based on my desire to quickly eliminate discomfort. In my rush for closure, many Clearheaders wondered about my insistence on resolution—and about what other problems I'd *not* heard along the way.

Confirmation Bias

Another extremely common "shortcut" we take is to favor the data that validates our preconceived assumptions. *"Confirmation bias" causes us to filter results or outcomes through what we want the outcome to be,* rather than observing facts with clarity. The more closely you listen for something in particular, the less you hear everything else. And frequently, the problem most worth solving or the best solution possible is sitting among the "everything else."

That can be difficult to see when we're under pressure—and when is an entrepreneur not under pressure? In those moments we tend to make assumptions, draw conclusions, and take shortcuts. Sometimes, that approach works. Often, in business, we even get rewarded for it. For example, I remember working on the redesign of the global site navigation for a major furniture retailer. We had ninety days. Thirty days to figure out the problem, thirty days to design a prototype for a solution, and another thirty days to test our hypothesis. And we did it. Ninety days from kickoff, the new nav was live.

But in the coming days, as we looked at our data, we didn't like what we saw. Our solution didn't appear to be any more successful than the control. For all our activity, we hadn't really gained any ground for our client.

While I knew that we had listened, I was certain that we'd not listened enough. We had understood some of the problems—specifically for returning customers and experienced furniture shoppers. But we'd entirely missed out on everyone else. Additionally, we'd presumed that shopping for a lamp, a rug, or a sofa was pretty much the same experience. We were not aware of the fast path that certain customers expected for the company's "hero products"—those popular, well-understood items that people simply added to carts and checked out with, as though they were buying milk at the grocery store. We'd taken several shortcuts based on other clients we had, our own assumptions about furniture, and what the client was leaning toward to begin with. And those shortcuts routed customers away from the staples of furniture shopping: rugs and sofas. We had not effectively listened.

As the ninety-day mark approached, we desperately wanted our new variation to outperform the control. We'd worked so hard, and the client had invested a lot of money with us. Everyone was hopeful. But with each passing day, it became clearer that the results were not what anyone wanted to hear. We had to resist the intense pull of confirmation bias and face facts: we'd created more problems than we'd solved.

Mechanized Thinking

Businesses often fall for the listening shortcut of rushing to the obvious solution or the obvious problem. This approach comes from our tendency toward mechanized thinking—*the notion that what worked before will work again*. Mechanized thinking can be a valuable way to handle basic rote tasks. It's a good thing we don't have to relearn how to hammer a nail every time we need to do it, for example. But this approach can fall short when it narrows our capacity not only to solve problems but to even identify them.

Mechanized thinking is insidious, as well—the more competent we become at a task, the more mechanized our thinking will become. And paradoxically, this often leads us to ill-fitting solutions and hypotheses. When we get in this sort of groove, we tend to grab the first obvious solution that presents itself to us. In fact, the solution may seem so obvious as to feel unquestionable. The thing is, the first response to solving a problem is rarely the best one. This apparent paradox is so common it has a name—the Einstellung effect.

The Einstellung effect holds that our initial solution hypotheses will almost always resemble the last one we created—regardless of how similar or different the problem actually is.

Most entrepreneurs are not rewarded for leaning back and listening. We're rewarded for being problem solvers. For moving forward. And moving fast. That's the archetype of a winner in business. It's an archetype that is celebrated for its occasional validity, but it's an archetype that stunts us and our companies. We have to be intentional if we want to operate differently.

Hypermediation

If it has long been a challenge for humans to openly, actively listen, it's only getting harder in a world where texts, alerts, headlines, streaming services, podcasts, and more compete for our attention all the time, everywhere we go. Add on the fractionalization of time and fragmentation of information through politics, programming, and marketing, and we can see how the modern world is essentially supercharging our biases.

Our world is flooded with algorithms that take advantage of our desires for gratification and closure. I write this not as a technophobe or a cynic but as a statement of fact and as a technological imperative. People today have easier and faster access to what they want than ever before. That can feel gratifying and beneficial, but it also leads to disorientation. We become overwhelmed by the paradox of choice. There's too much information and too many potential perspectives. Our brains are simply not capable of taking in all that information, assimilating and reconciling it, and knowing what to do with it. We're all desperate for ways to make sense of too much information too quickly and that leads us to lean into our natural biases without actually listening and absorbing all the potential options.

You know how it goes. "If you *like* this," the world tells you, "then you'll *love* that." "Come with us down this path, and come now," they beckon. "Don't worry about where those other roads might go; they're unfamiliar. Unsafe." If we stay in our silos, we can escape the discomfort of uncertainty.

It's true that when we only hear things that sound familiar, we experience a tremendous amount of comfort. Echo chambers provide this comfort; they are psychological, intellectual, or technical places or situations where everything we see and hear sounds familiar and reinforces our existing beliefs. That may feel good, but when we stay in these spaces, we degrade the capacity to listen openly. We increasingly become able to hear only certain things the longer we're in that echo chamber. *Echo chambers are the enemies of growth.* And it would be no exaggeration to say that a growing percentage of the modern world is living in deep echo chambers.

We don't know where the bottom of this is—the extent to which contrary information can be so discomforting as to be demonizing and affirming information can be so gratifying as to be lionizing. Between the physiological and the psychological, it can feel like the world around us is unendingly stymieing our attempts to build our listening skills. And that might be true. But that doesn't make it impossible.

Tuning In

Recognizing our inability to listen and acknowledging we have the capacity to develop this skill is an essential starting point toward healthy growth. But cultivating this skill does not happen quickly— nor should it.

Like every human on the planet, I have been practicing listening for years. In fact, I've probably logged decades of overtime. As a young introvert, I was constantly listening to music—just me and my handy boom box, occasionally with headphones—every hour I was not in school. For many years in adolescence, I was something of a wallflower who stood back and just listened, taking it all in. It was a skill I cultivated unintentionally. In fact, I probably viewed it as a defect, as a sign that I was not out doing things with other people. But later in life, when I became an entrepreneur, I found it served me incredibly well.

As a founder, I would go into a room of teammates, investors, or clients, and my natural inclination was to listen before I spoke. And when that didn't suit the occasion, I would start by asking questions to orient myself to the people around me. What were they hoping to get from this meeting or conversation? What was their story? Where were they from? How were we alike? How were we different? Taking the initiative to ask questions is a common entrepreneurial trait, but the skill of listening to the responses and determining what to do with that information was something that definitely took practice.

All of that said, I still had a lot to learn about listening. For instance, I had to learn who to listen to, where to point my metaphorical ears. In my Insound days, I have to admit, it didn't occur to me to listen to customers. It sounds naive now, but at the time, web design didn't really bring customers into the equation until right before products went to market. Today, we take for granted that we should do usability research, listen to the voice of the customer, and so on. But back in 1997, my ears were simply not open to what the customer really desired. The assuredness I had in my ideas was not built on sufficient evidence, because I didn't have that evidence. I wasn't listening for it.

To truly listen, we need to cultivate openness, but we also need to tune our listening. We want to take in the stimuli, but we have to also discern veracity and proportionality. When we go to a concert, for example, we set ourselves up to hear the performance we want to hear. To do that, we have to block out our own noise. We have to block out crowd noise. We have to allow ourselves to focus on the music in spite of all the distractions.

The same is true in business. We need to get from distracting noise to clear signals. We have to lean out to be open to the information, but then we need to tune in to the most salient matters.

For healthy growth, the most salient matters originate from those three moments of revelation: the core desires, the problems most worth solving, and the best hypotheses to solve those problems.

In many ways, that's what we've been doing here, together, up until now. We've been leaning out and deliberately availing ourselves of new information so that we can confidently accelerate toward our desired outcomes. And so, having laid the groundwork, here's where we transition from the "why" (growth) and "how" (listening) to the "what" of this book. If we were in a yoga class, having shared our intentions, centered our breath, and warmed up, we'd be ready to start our poses and sequences. We'd be ready to practice. In this book, our version of "yoga for growth" is a practice that we call GPS.

PART II

practicing growth

chapter 4

The Antidote: GPS

Sometime around 2006, I was doing work for Toyota. As part of our engagement, I had the chance to sit in on a couple of "Toyota University" classes in California. It was there that I was first introduced to "The Toyota Way" and concepts of Lean manufacturing. I'd no prior exposure to *kaizen* (continuous improvement) or *obeyas* (command centers) or how businesses thought about optimizing for product-market fit. I recall being intellectually stimulated by the classes. It was all so thoughtful and logical, and it provided a great sense of purpose and order. But I never fully bought in. It felt a little dogmatic. Maybe even cultish. "The Toyota Way!" I semi-scoffed. Its name implied both superiority and the acknowledgment that there were other "ways."

All my life I've resisted doctrine. I'm not religious. I'm not a club joiner. And though I've dabbled in many business and entrepreneurship methodologies, I've never fully committed to one. Six Sigma felt too mechanical and lacking in empathy for me. The Theory of Constraints seemed light in the areas of experimentation and optimization. There was Agile and BPM and EOS and others I perused, sampled, or bumped into over the years. I took a little something away from each and carried the learnings forward. It's probably the cynic in me, but I simply did not believe that any of these methodologies *really* worked.

When I first read *The Lean Startup*, however, it felt different. The year 2011 was a perfect storm for me—my drive to start a new company aligned with a startup framework that sounded both topical and pragmatic. For one, it operated on several levels—the experience, the product, and the startup itself. But the message of *The Lean Startup* was also extremely timely. It helped me organize my own thinking around design and experimentation at the exact moment when businesses were making the push to become more user-centric and data-driven. This book hit the shelves during an explosion of research, experimentation, and analytics SaaS in the market.

No surprise then that Clearhead was founded, in part, because of how much Ryan and I admired *The Lean Startup*. It was the first system I truly bought into. And it would be some time before I saw its limitations.

What Is GPS, *Really?*

"GPS" is an acronym for "Goals Problems Solutions." On a basic level, it is a framework for entrepreneurship and growth that provides more predictable, satisfying outcomes. It's also a mode of design thinking that is evidence-based and performance-oriented. And it's an operating system comprehensive enough to guide design, operations, and leadership. Above all, and like yoga, *GPS is a practice. It never ends. It's never perfect.* There is a sense of play in the system. But over time, when we practice GPS, we get better at solving those problems that stand in between us and what we desire.

GPS consists of six "poses" that, if followed sequentially and practiced consistently, lead to healthy growth: Desires, Goals, Problems, Hypotheses, Experiments, and Outcomes.

DESIRES GOALS PROBLEMS HYPOTHESES EXPERIMENTS OUTCOMES

Like all great art, GPS steals liberally—from Lean, Constraints, Agile, Kaizen, The Five Whys, and other frameworks. For the rest of this book, we'll review in great detail how to practice GPS. We will describe why each step of the practice exists; how to proceed through each step; how to listen along the way; and how to put it all together, operationalize it, and sustain it. But keep in mind, as with yoga, there is no one right way to practice GPS. *So long as each of the poses is earnestly confronted, you are "doing" GPS.*

When we founded Clearhead in 2012, we were fully agile and lean but had not yet conceived of GPS. We were early to market with the idea of using A/B testing software to guide design decisions beyond landing pages. We wanted to take experimentation out of the dark corners of performance marketing and analytics and inject it more broadly into experience and product design.

We had embraced the Lean mantras that fast failures are better than slow ones, that the speed of learning is a measure of success, and that every test is a winner. It seemed self-evident: Whether you win or lose, you're learning. You're getting closer to the next, better hypothesis.

But as I previewed in Chapter 2, we also sensed that something wasn't quite right: more often than not, our hypotheses were not being validated. And so we began to pick at our assumptions about where good ideas came from. Yes, on some level, they came from good hypotheses. But where did good hypotheses come from? In time, we came to realize that the most successful hypotheses—where the outcomes were positive and statistically significant—were those where a clear problem was understood, clearly articulated, and sufficiently addressed. *Problems. That was where good hypotheses came from.*

With this realization, we knew we needed to revisit and redesign our process to center around problems. Rather than sprinting into hypotheses, we needed to turn our ears back toward problems. We needed to lean out and listen before we tuned in.

Essentially, we were flipping our original process on its head. We had been so focused on hypotheses and testing that we weren't devoting enough time to understanding the problems. And though I'd never said it out loud before, that was the root of my discomfort with Lean. It did not spend enough time with "The Why" or "The Constraints." It was too meta for me—too abstracted from resources and opportunity cost. With our new approach at Clearhead, we were spending more time focusing on goals and problems and less on hypotheses. It felt like a risk. It felt contrary to how most every business operated. But also, maybe that's why it felt so right.

Through these insights and through the efforts of our entire team to redesign our work model, "Problem Solution Mapping" was born. "Problem Solution Mapping," or "PSM" for short, was the method that we would eventually rename "GPS."

While we were developing our new framework, Clearhead's competition was growing. We were no longer one of the very few companies promising better design through experimentation. Copycat agencies were popping up, and larger, preexisting agencies had begun promising optimization as a service. Fortunately, we now had a way to differentiate ourselves. We were raising our hand and saying, "We're calling bullshit on the industry. We're questioning Lean. And we're rejecting the 'test everything' hype."

It was a very contrarian marketing technique, but it was also very effective, largely because it was authentic. Ryan and I deeply believed in GPS. GPS may have been born as a design thinking methodology, but we soon realized this framework was just as applicable to internal business processes. We lived GPS in every aspect of our business. We ate the dog food and drank the champagne. GPS became a unifying practice for everyone at Clearhead.

We modeled it for our clients so well because we practiced it internally, every day.

With the development of GPS, annual planning at Clearhead changed, quarterly business reviews changed, town hall presentations changed, meeting agendas changed, the employee review process changed. We designed GPS templates in our task-tracking software (Asana), in Google Docs, and in Slack. Every conversation was reframed through the relationship between Desires, Goals, Problems, Hypotheses, Experiments, and Outcomes. At every meeting at Clearhead, we were using the same vernacular—the same metadata. If you eavesdropped on a Clearhead meeting, you'd hear something like this:

- What does the client most desire for this product?
- How will we know if we have succeeded?
- What problem are we solving?
- Is it the root problem?
- Is it the problem most worth solving?
- What evidence do we have?
- What's our hypothesis?
- What outcome do we expect from solving this problem?
- Why do we believe that?
- Again, what evidence do we have?

GPS changed more than our conversations. It changed our priorities. Like many service companies, Clearhead originally organized our employees' work around billable hours. Our steadfast focus on billability, however, obscured deeper problems related to operations, human resources, or service quality. What about recruitment? What about org structure? What about benefits? What about bonuses? What about work–life balance? What about time spent identifying those problems? Were they not problems most worth solving?

And so we asked ourselves the very same questions we demanded that our clients answer: What did we desire most as a business? What were our goals across a balanced scorecard? What were our problems most worth solving? We began at the top, from an enterprise perspective. And then we worked our way across and down and back up again, systematically practicing GPS internally in the same way we did for our clients' user experience and product designs. For every department, we asked our teams to explicitly define goals and the problems that were preventing us from achieving those goals. And we didn't stop there. For every role, we created space—and processes—for people to identify problems and to research and work on them collaboratively.

Method, Not Madness

To be clear, designing and implementing this practice was hard work. It required all of us—but especially our leadership team—to rethink most of what we knew about management and decision-making. Right away, though, GPS was embraced throughout the company. Everyone intuitively knew it made sense. Moreover, they knew that the alternative—working faster, working more, going with your gut—was untenable. Teammates would repeatedly share that, whereas every other place they'd worked felt like madness, Clearhead felt like method.

While it was not difficult to get buy-in, it was still challenging to get people to slow their momentum and not leap toward ideas. Old habits die hard. Not a day went by when people didn't fall back on old methods—"can't you just let me brainstorm?" Or "can't you just let us skip to the obvious conclusion?"

No. No we couldn't. Many times I wanted to, but *implementing GPS required all of us to shift to a whole new way of thinking and acting.* It required completely redesigning our delivery processes, even when clients perceived our changes as adding extra steps. But we were all in. Because if our goal was growth and our problem was excessive failure, then our solution hypothesis required that we better understand "why we fail." As the title of Ryan Holiday's book suggests, *The Obstacle Is the Way*.

As a founder, using GPS meant relinquishing control and trusting the practice, which sometimes felt impossible. It was exactly the opposite of the hyperfunctioning approach I'd frequently taken, where I was a main touch point on everything happening with the business. *With GPS, I had to trust my people—not to be right all the time but to follow the practice.* I had defined the constraints, the objectives, and the rules we were operating under, and then I had to let it go. Early and often, that felt uncomfortable. But many years and literally hundreds of business cases later, I can confirm that GPS works—for the institution *and* the entrepreneur.

GPS is also incredibly flexible. It can be basic or ornate. For all its structure, GPS doesn't preclude play or surprise. GPS is methodological in that there are prescribed areas of concentration (Desires, Goals, Problems, Hypotheses, Experiments, and Outcomes), but what you do within those constraints assumes a great deal of freedom. It allows for various degrees of rigor, fidelity, and personalization. And while it is deliberate, it is faster in speed to value (rather than speed to market) than whatever methodology you are presently employing. By focusing on problems before solutions, it neutralizes the inefficiencies of never-ending debate, noise, and bias.

By 2017, many of the largest companies in America wanted to work with Clearhead primarily because of GPS—because they understood Lean and Agile but agreed that our practice would lead them to better design outcomes. Simultaneously, we'd grown over 100 percent every year we were in business and had managed to retain over 90 percent of our employees. More than anything I'd ever accomplished professionally, that felt like healthy growth.

chapter 5

Desires

Like many entrepreneurs, I would be considered "goal-oriented."
When I started Clearhead in 2012, I actually had a revenue size,
profit margin percentage, employee count, and time horizon in
mind. I even wrote those goals down for myself before day one of
operations. Having been at the beginning of a startup before, I knew
it was going to be a demanding journey. That 24-7, 365 feeling of
sprinting a marathon was familiar to me. What was different this
time, and different from most startups and most entrepreneurs, was
that I achieved all of my goals. All of them. In fact, better and faster
than I'd imagined.

And yet, I felt dissatisfied.

This dissatisfaction, in turn, caused me to ask two questions that
I wished I'd asked at the outset: (1) Where do I go after I meet my
stated goals? And (2) Why were these my goals to begin with?

Until then, I hadn't had the space or time to consider either question. I had spent seven years of my life knee-deep in Clearhead. For
those seven years, I had been in constant motion, sleeping very
little, spending most of the week in meetings and much of the rest

going to and from airports. All the while, I was trying to model excellence, make constant improvements, and maintain some semblance of health.

I fit in family and my personal life wherever I could. I did a great deal of the work getting Clearhead off the ground while moving with my wife and two infant daughters. Our third child arrived not too long after we launched. As a result of my travel, I adapted to coming home and immediately moving into hyperdrive. I wasn't capable of just hanging out as part of my family because I felt compelled to make the most of the limited time I had with them. In my attempts to make up for precious, lost time, I did what I learned through my startups—I did more, faster.

After exiting Clearhead, *I realized the vexing truth: this was not how I wanted to live.* And yet, it was the way I had built my life. I had been extremely intentional about it. I was, by any measure, good at it. My life and the role I was playing in it certainly had provided rewards. But I had this nagging sense that my life was getting away from me, that my role as an entrepreneur was pulling me away from my true desires. This deep and troubling thought inspired an even deeper and more troubling one: I had no idea what I most, truly desired.

Where Do We Go from Here?

This was not a question that I was able to resolve while we were building Clearhead. In fact, it was not something I confronted during the two years after we sold the company. Some of the delay probably had to do with the challenges of changing direction and slowing momentum. But I think more of it has to do with the nature of Desire—its elusiveness, its mystery, and its accompanying shame.

It took so much time to understand the gap between what I had been doing and what I most deeply desired, at least in part, because what I had been doing appeared to be working spectacularly well. Clearhead was an incredible success. Our work was good. Our people were great. We were making money hand over fist. We were winning awards. I should have been enjoying every moment of it.

Instead of feeling successful, however, I felt empty. Oftentimes, our best days felt like my worst days. When we'd win new accounts, I'd think mostly of the meetings and travel that they'd require. When we'd hire new people, I'd fear that I was getting stretched too thin and that I could not give them enough support. When we announced the sale of the company to the team, I cried from the sense that I had committed an act of betrayal.

The more successful my startup became, the more depleted I felt. I had less energy and felt less healthy. On the surface, all of the KPIs were pointing in the right direction—toward growth. But inside, the indicator lights were flashing. My experience is familiar to many entrepreneurs—we tend to default to hyperfunctioning when we're in the thick of things. But this feeling of depletion went even deeper. Things were missing that I couldn't articulate. I felt that the increasingly successful entrepreneur I had become was a ways away from the person I was meant to be. The faster my startup had grown, the more I felt like I was stunted. Surely, that couldn't be healthy, could it?

It was not until the summer of 2019, when I was with my family in the resplendent Mad River Valley of Vermont, that I was able to reckon with myself. After a grueling final year, and with one foot out of the door at Accenture, who had acquired us two years before, I began to get the same question over and over: "So, what's next?" I did not know what was next, but I knew what I would *not* be doing. I would not be founding another high-growth startup. I was done. I wouldn't do it again. I couldn't. I didn't have it in me.

That much was crystal clear. The uncertainty of my professional future, however, begged the question I'd asked myself many times before: what are my goals? For the first time in my life, I had no answer but rather a fast follow-on question: *where do goals even come from?*

That was the question! The question I'd never asked before. I'd asked where good outcomes come from. And where good experiments come from. I'd done the same with hypotheses and problems. But I stopped at goals. I never really understood where good goals came from. Until one day, while I was walking in those hills of Vermont, the answer became obvious. SMART (Specific, Measurable, Actionable, Realistic, and Timely) goals are born from core desires. And while I had achieved every goal I set out for at Clearhead, I'd never spent the time to define what I most desired and whether my goals were a fair measure of those desires.

At the end of my Clearhead journey, it was finally time to go back to the beginning.

What Are Desires, *Really*?

Entrepreneurs have desires. So do startups. And what I've come to learn is that it is the relationship between these desires—those of the entrepreneur and their startup—that ultimately determines if and how something grows.

The word "desire" has a slightly negative connotation. It often conjures associations of lust or avarice. And for many reasons— some good and some not so good—we're frequently conditioned to separate our desires from our professional lives. When we're acting in a professional capacity, we almost automatically mediate ourselves from our desires because thinking about what we desire feels aggressive, or even shameful. There's no "I" in "team," right?

But not only is this not necessary; it isn't even helpful. *An entrepreneur's desires should be integrated into the desires of their startup.* Those desires should inspire and inform their goals.

Desire is a yearning deeply connected to who you are in the world. Desires are born from both your genetics and your socialization. They are not immovable, but they are deeply rooted. *They are, ideally, what sets us in motion. They provide us with an honest purpose.*

Now, the kind of desire I'm talking about isn't the salacious kind. I'm not arguing for sex at the office or Ayn Rand's "Objectivism." Instead, I am suggesting we get to the root motivations that drive you and your business. Stripped of artifice, stripped of pretense, what do you most desire in life—professionally and personally?

The repression of desire is what leads to dissatisfaction, regression, and even in the best cases, unhealthy growth. On some level, the "Great Resignation" that we witnessed in 2021 was precipitated by a delta between employees' work life and their deeper, personal desires. Although startups can fulfill many desires—for intellectual stimulation and validation, for instance—*the role of entrepreneur is frequently at odds with other, basic human desires of physical wellness, intimacy, free play, etc.* When we start with the wrong goals—goals that don't nourish our true desires—bad things happen. We suppress our feelings. We hyperfunction. We self-medicate. We regret. Inversely, there can only be healthy growth in business when its outward success is aligned to inner desires. And of course, alignment starts with the founder—the entrepreneur.

Spiting your nose to save your face is rarely a good business decision. *In startups, as in all healthy relationships, desires have to be mutually fulfilling.* Not equally. Not perfectly. But mutually.

All that sounds great—except most of us don't know what we desire. And we've been told either that it doesn't matter or that it's a private matter. If you're an entrepreneur, you've had it drilled into you that the important thing is the rapid and oversized growth of your business. You must do *everything* possible to keep it afloat, at worst, and racing forward, ideally. If you're a successful entrepreneur, your identity has become tightly linked to all you did to get from there to here. But what if those societal pressures know nothing about there and here? What if focusing solely on the business means you're leaving out a whole dimension of your life? Or multiple dimensions?

I know that in some ways, it feels impossible to solve this riddle. And I also know that it's not. I am in no way suggesting "we can have it all." But I am confirming that "we can have so much more." You can discover what you most desire as a human being who is also an entrepreneur, which will in turn lead to fundamental discoveries for your startup. And you can pursue both of those things in concert, intentionally, deciding exactly where you want to spend your time and resources. But pursue them separately at your peril—to reach a truly satisfying outcome, there must be a through line from your personal desires to those of your startup.

Why Desires?

I would not argue with you if you suggested that all of this talk about desire has a "new age" whiff about it. You might rightfully even roll your eyes when I suggest that "desires" are like "intentions" in yoga—they set forth a hope and a direction for your practice. I do think that's an apt analogy, but rest assured, I am talking about desires for wholly practical reasons. I am obsessed with defining and unpacking desire because I know how it can very directly, very practically impact growth for entrepreneurs and their startups.

So what does a startup desire? How is that different from what it needs? Fundamentally, a business *needs* to make more money than it loses or have sufficient capital to offset its spending. It *needs* to have the resources to execute. It also *needs* to work within the constraints of law. These are not desires. These are existential needs. A business cannot exist—at least not for any length of time—without these things.

Businesses presume those existential needs, but they are functionally built on desires. The desires to be successful, to beat the competition, to create an excellent product, to impact people's lives. Meeting the status quo will not fulfill these deeper desires. And so, we must ask: Which of those desires matter most? And why? Those answers suggest the inextricable link between the founder's desires and the business's desires.

We see evidence of this link all the time—in a business's mission statements, vision statements, and organizational values. Many businesses do ask the foundational questions: What are we? Why do we exist? What do we wish to accomplish? What do we fundamentally value? What do we want to model in our behavior? *Good mission, vision, and values statements function as distillations of the business's desires,* oftentimes as imagined through the lens of the founder and their desires.

Honestly, for most of my career as a founder, I didn't think much of missions and visions. They felt like obligations of marketing and human resources more than actual agents of purpose or growth. I came to see their critical importance, however, when I first heard Simon Sinek's talk about the importance of focusing on "The Why." At the risk of reducing a wonderful and far-reaching set of ideas to two sentences, *Start with the Why* convinced me that it is purpose that drives the "How" and "What" of a business. Similarly, it is inspiration and not manipulation of force that leads to greater achievement.

With that new perspective, I concluded that mission, vision, and values are essential for scale, which is essential for healthy growth. Honestly, they're sort of like desire, dressed up and made up for the close-up. They're not sufficient on their own, but if steeped in the core desires of the organization, they can help align institutional desires with the desires of the entrepreneur. When aligned, you can nourish your startup and your startup can nourish you.

Dimensions of Desire

The desires of an entrepreneur are, of course, not exactly the same as those of a company. So let's first separate entrepreneurial desires (which are personal) from those of the startup (which are institutional). *Personal entrepreneurial desires are the elements of life that we profoundly want because they nourish us physiologically and emotionally.* They might be aligned to professional success, but they do not necessarily need to be. Beneath the title, entrepreneurs are just human beings. Like teachers, lawyers, or doctors, they must align their personal desires with the work they do. The dimensions of desire are the same; the difference is to what extent they align or diverge from the startups they form and lead.

Though it is frequently not the case, it stands to reason that desires should map to goals if you want to grow toward your desires. In simple terms, *goals should define the outcomes you most desire.* To that end, we can plot all desires—for ourselves and for our startups—on a pentagon.

The five dimensions of an entrepreneur's personal desire are these:

1. **Physical desire:** How do we want to feel in our bodies? This includes our appearance, our health, and our sexuality. Be warned, this dimension is frequently subject to uncomfortable feelings of shame or vanity. Without considering our physical desires, however, we risk putting our startups ahead of our health and wellness.

2. **Emotional desire:** How do we want to feel in our hearts and minds? This dimension relates to our mental and emotional state and our own personal tendencies toward introversion or extroversion, for example. This dimension also encompasses our closest and most fundamental relationships, such as our spouse or partner, our immediate family, and our children—the people we are most vulnerable and authentic with in our lives.

3. **Social desire:** How do we want to be seen and considered publicly? This dimension includes how we exist out in the world. It includes our relationships and connections

beyond the emotional realm. This would be friends, peers, colleagues, and other connections—each moving farther out in terms of closeness.

4. **Material desire:** What do we want to have? Material desires are our needs for income, wealth, status, and assets. This is one of the hardest to differentiate between what we actually desire and what the world around us tries to convince us of.

5. **Experiential desire:** How do we want to live? Our experiential desires are those that correlate to how we exist in the world, and the relationships we have with things larger than ourselves. These desires include our needs for travel, adventure, learning, and life experience. They also account for our spirituality or religious beliefs, for those who are so inclined.

The five dimensions of a startup's institutional desire are these:

1. **Intrinsic desire:** What does the business fundamentally desire to be(come)? This is where you define the thing that you are creating. Is it a product, a service, an experience, a retailer, a media platform? Is it something else?

2. **Functional desire:** What needs does the business desire to fill? The functional desire of a business defines how it provides benefits to customers, employees, the community, and to society and the world.

3. **Social desire:** What position in the market does the business wish to occupy? This dimension relates to how the business is perceived in the world. What is the business's addressable market, target customer, and competitive advantage?

4. **Developmental desire:** What does growth look like for this business? Here, we describe the company's financial performance and operations. Will it have high margins,

low margins, or no margins? What is the pace of growth the business wants? The size of the business? What is the sourcing of funding? Is it meant to be self-sustaining? Is it meant to be sold one day? Should it go public?

5. **Experiential desire:** What sort of experience will this business engender for its employees (including its founder)? This is where culture and work–life balance are defined. Is this the sort of business that is tightly knit, in a physical location? Or is it more distributed and fluid? Is it the sort of company that feels like a family? Are days all work and no play? Are they work hard and play hard?

As with entrepreneurs and their startups, products and design have desires as well. They deeply want to be some things and not others. But for the purposes of this book, we'll focus on the entrepreneur and their company. To create positive, forward momentum within GPS, an entrepreneur must first define their personal desires and then do the same for their startup. *The more closely aligned the two are, the more likely that growth will be mutual and healthy.* To get there, it all starts with listening.

Listening for Our Desires

For the next five chapters—the parts of this book that detail the practice of GPS—we will focus on startups rather than on the personal desires of their founders. But right here, right now, we are starting with you, the entrepreneur. There will always be billion-dollar exits, and unicorns, and celebrity tech stars, but rarely will you find a happy, healthy person in that role. Worse, there are millions more of our kind, lost, wasted, or broken on the side of the road, who never knew what they most desired to begin with. To avoid that ending, we must begin with the human side of entrepreneurship.

Listening for desires is perhaps the most challenging part of GPS.
Some of this has to do with the honesty and intimacy it requires
and the shame and repression it bumps into. But equally, it's difficult
because it is a "cold start." Everything that follows in GPS follows
on or pivots from some previous pose. But desires are where it all
starts. So if at first it seems difficult or unnatural, do not fret. As with
all practices, there is no best. Do not let perfection be the enemy of
great.

Begin simply by getting quiet. This is not work to be done in an
office or among friends or peers. Go someplace where you can hear
yourself. Then, begin with those personal, entrepreneurial desires.
Go one dimension at a time. Ask yourself:

"What do I most desire [physically, emotionally, etc.]?"

You will have many answers. You might start with high-level
desires, but that's not where you'll end. For each one, *ask yourself
why you want that.* Then ask why again, until there is no answer or
because the answer is, "I just do." For example, you might begin by
saying your physical desire is to lose weight or add muscles or have
a better sex life. Great. But why do you want those things? Is it about
vanity? Love? Is it about living longer? Resist self-judgment. If it is
about vanity, that's fine. Shame and repression are the enemies of
desire. *Try to get to the core of the desire in a single sentence.* Better
yet, maybe you can get it to a single headline phrase, followed by a
short sentence descriptor. One of my physical desires is #sustained-
mobility (as you'll see, GPS is hashtag friendly). I desire #sustained-
mobility because I want to be able to travel and play with my family
for as long as humanly possible.

Similarly, my core material desire has never been to "make a billion dollars" or "get rich." Rarely is the desire for the thing itself.
It's almost always for something beyond that thing. Far beneath the
accumulation of wealth are other, deeper desires relating to safety,
time, providing, etc. My core material desire is #invaluable-time,
which has much more to do with how I value the "professional"

hours of my day than it does with compensation or assets. If you dig deeper, you will find your core desires for each dimension, just as I found mine.

To note, there can be multiple core desires for each dimension. That makes perfect sense. But endeavor to focus on the roots and not the leaves—on the source and not the symptoms. And if you discover that there are multiple roots and sources, that is great. *Jot them all down. Don't repress.* We'll sort out priorities shortly.

As you take stock of your desires, stay true. Capture those things that might sound embarrassing or unpleasant. If you most desire validation from your peers, click into that. If you desire affection from your partner, don't resist. If you want to be the very best at something, own it. Desires are not democratic or meritocratic. *They are personal—you don't need anyone's permission to feel the way you feel.*

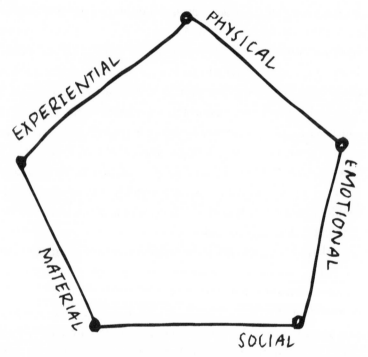

When you think you are done, you may have five core desires—one for each dimension. Realistically, however, you will have more, and they will not line up perfectly. Ask yourself if any of them should be combined or relocated to another dimension. Then when you are satisfied that there are no duplicates, that they are all core desires, and that they are properly organized, ask yourself: "If I had $100 to spend on my desires, how would I allocate the money?" Anything that you would not spend more than $1 on is probably not a desire that will define or restrict future growth. Make note of it. File it away in the notes or comments section. And then remove it from the pentagon. What remains is what you, the entrepreneur, most desire in life. Frame it. Laminate it. Bookmark it. Whatever you need to do. Just don't lose sight of it.

Listening to Our Startup's Desires

It's not merely my own personal desires that I have betrayed over the years; I've also risked the desires of my startups. It was 2000, and we were a growing Insound—by then, a beloved indie music web store. We wanted to build on our initial success. If we were going to survive, we needed to grow. And so we decided we should become the source of "everything indie." We started "Insound Cinema," hired indie film aficionados, and started acquiring, selling, and streaming under-distributed indie films. It was a brand-new e-commerce market, adjacent to our original one. We figured that it made perfect sense. Does that sound familiar?

But putting all of our attention on something shiny and new only served to starve our core business desires. Our foray into film obscured our ability to see the shortcomings of what we were already doing in indie music. We lost sight of our customer, our product, and our brand. We spent a lot of time and resources chasing a perceived added benefit that really only served to distract us from where our focus should have been.

Businesses and organizations face immense pressure to focus their attention toward the desires of others at the expense of their own. I saw this all the time at Clearhead, where many of our SaaS partners got pulled away from their core desires and toward either the whims of the market or their competitors' latest features. Many companies gave into these pressures, shifting their focus, and allowing their true goals to fall by the wayside. A/B testing products became Personalization platforms which became Machine Learning companies or User Experience companies. The compulsion to be good at what others wanted often came at the expense of what they most fundamentally desired.

Believe it or not, the process for *listening to your startup's desires is not all that different from the work you just did for yourself.* One key difference, however, is that many startups have already, well, started up. If your startup has not yet been born, then...great timing. Stop what you are doing and define your institutional desires. Do not pass go. But if your startup is already a thing—if you've received investment or built an MVP or you are already conducting business—then it might *seem* like a different story. The thought of defining or possibly rewriting the core purpose of a startup after the fact can seem academic or even futile. But trust me, it is not. GPS is a practice, and we are at the beginning, not the end. *By defining and aligning desires between you and your startup now, we will shine light on smarter goals, clearer problems, and more-likely-to-succeed hypotheses.* Moreover, we will be more likely to engender healthy growth through the titration of entrepreneurial and institutional desires.

Once again, as the founder, this is your responsibility. If you have partners, especially equal or plurality partners, you must work through this together. But remember that institutional desires should not be written by a committee. They need to be written by those who conceived of the business and created its initial equity. The entire company doesn't vote on them. Customers don't rate or review them. When the time comes, you can hire a consultant or an agency to translate these desires into mission, vision, and value statements. But that time is not now.

On the other hand, if your startup is already active and you have written those statements—great, gather them. Ideally, they will serve as inspiration for this work. In the worst cases, however, you may end up realizing you need to tear those statements up and start over. But better that than lying to yourself about what your startup really is.

This is probably a great moment to confirm—in case it is not obvious—that I am using the terms "startup" and "founder" very broadly in this chapter. If you are a digital executive with startup expectations, or if you are the creator of a new product inside an established business, the very same principles apply, albeit with the constraints of the institution's mission, vision, and values. *Your established company requires "The Why" for healthy growth. So does your department. So does your product.* You may not work for a startup, and you may not be in a position to define the mission and vision for your company, but you can still practice GPS and you can still listen for the desires of your startup inside the enterprise.

And so whether you are a tech startup founder or the chief digital officer at some fast-moving brand, find that quiet space. Look at the dimensions of institutional desire—Intrinsic, Functional, Social, Developmental, and Experiential. Now ask yourself those same questions about your startup. This time, however, instead of asking "why," ask: "Is it clear?" "Is it true?" "Is that what it truly desires to be?" For example, what does your startup intrinsically desire to be? The answer is not "a unicorn" or "the best headless CMS on the planet." It is more elemental than that. Are you building a product? A brand? A service? A retailer? A platform? Be honest and precise and then add a word or phrase to qualify your startup's intrinsic desire (*"organic skin care* brand" or *"digital marketing software* product," etc.). Then stop. Just a few words is all you'll need.

Bear in mind, when startups resist their intrinsic desires, they frequently buckle. When software companies overinvest in services, they burn cash faster, neglect their product, and damage their valuation. When agencies attempt to become software companies, they almost always fail. Be true about what you are and what you are not.

Continue, one dimension at a time. What function does your startup serve? Be as bold, but as specific and honest, as possible. Where do you desire to exist in the market? Is it a high-end product? Is it more of a commodity? Is it an aspirational brand? A friendly one? A simple, utilitarian one? Are you a market leader or a follower? The only wrong answers are the insincere ones.

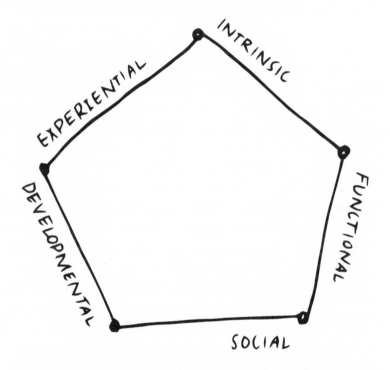

As you go through each dimension, look for contradictions. It is hard to fathom, for instance, an online grocery business that is also a very high-margin business. Similarly, it's hard to imagine an e-commerce loyalty software that exists to feed the planet. A certain logic should flow from dimension to dimension.

Again, there may be more than one desire for each dimension. That is completely normal. But when you have exhausted the questions and refined and combined your answers, ask yourself that same question we asked before: "If I had $100 to spend on these desires, how would I allocate it?" Those desires that look like "nice to haves" are probably just that. Once you're done writing, refining, and (loosely) prioritizing, get those single sentence descriptions or hashtags down. It's time to line up the personal with the institutional.

Aligning Desires

When you are done, you will have two pentagons with desires inscribed for each of the five dimensions. Maybe they look something like this:

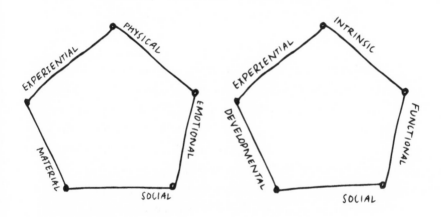

Great work. Excellent practice. Now take another look at your two pentagons. Place one on top of the other. The institutional one nested inside the personal one. The personal one nested inside the institutional one. How do they look? Are your desires aligned? Are they conflicted?

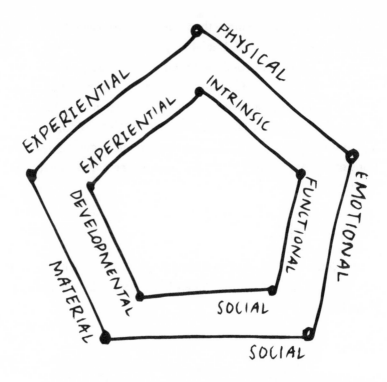

From experience, I know the many areas of potential friction. With my desires fully delineated, I realized pretty quickly that my role as an outgoing entrepreneur was at odds with my introverted need for time and space to myself. Similarly, I recognized that sitting at a desk or on a plane all the time didn't line up at all with my desire to maintain my mobility. And that the lifestyle my business appeared to demand of me also made it nearly impossible to fulfill my desire to have more shared experiences with my wife. Finally, I came to discover that my personal desire for wealth accumulation—my material desires—were more modest than the developmental desires of my hyper-growth agency. My pentagons were definitely out of alignment.

My point is not to suggest that there are land mines everywhere but rather to be mindful of the conflict from the outset. Do your pentagons nest nicely, like tidy Tupperware bowls? Or do you have to twist yourself to fit into your startup? Do you have to contort your startup to meet your needs? These tensions may be resolvable but only if you consider how the desires are or are not aligned. Looking at your pentagons, ask yourself, "Where is there conflict?" "What can I do to mitigate or overcome the conflict?" "What will happen if I cannot mitigate the conflict and some core desires are not fulfilled?"

What happens next does not necessarily need to be bigger, different, or on trend. *It does, however, need to demonstrate alignment between personal and institutional goals.* If you align these desires, no matter where your startup goes, you can't go too far off course. You now have a rudder to help you steer in the right direction.

Still, obstacles are destined to appear. They certainly did for me. But those desire pentagons can bring you back to what really matters for you.

Even after Clearhead. After GPS. After rediscovering my desires. Even after all that, I nearly tried to start a new business or two. While on sabbatical in bucolic Vermont, I began to fill my days by drafting multiple business plans and distracting myself. Of course I went there—hyperfunctioning, serial entrepreneurship was my default mode. And so early on in my "retirement," I began the process of developing a "hi-fi cafe" in Austin, where we live most of the year. I'd spent time in similar venues around the world—cafes where the music is supervised, frequently played on excellent stereo systems, and amplified in such a way to engender more listening than talking. I was a lifelong record collector. And I loved to work and spend time at "all-day cafes." It felt like a great fit for many of my desires and for the people in the city that I love. LA had a great one. So did New York. It seemed almost imperative that Austin—the "Live Music Capital of the World"—should have one.

Like many entrepreneurs, I saw a perceived need, and the wheels immediately started turning. I bought land. Yep. I designed the building. Sure did. I assembled a team. Uh-huh. But the closer we got to breaking ground, the more I realized that the project would starve more desires than it would nourish. I had just begun writing and exercising again—two things that I truly desired more of. I had begun mentoring other founders—something else I deeply wanted to do. I'd cleared out my calendar every day before 8:30 a.m. and after 3:30 p.m. so I could hang out with my family—the thing I most profoundly desired. And so when I finally drew that second pentagon, I knew that the two would not fit together.

My physical desires would be challenged by the seven days a week and late nights that are intrinsic to a hospitality business. The fulfillment I obtained from writing would not be possible during the formative stages of construction deadlines, staffing crises, and customer acquisition. I was either going to have to control my personal desires to fit the institutional ones, or I was going to struggle to nourish this new startup. My hi-fi cafe sure sounded nice. But the shapes didn't fit. I ended up selling the property and putting the business plan back up on the shelf. Maybe one day, when my desires shift, I'll take it back down. But not now.

chapter 6

Goals

Here's a familiar scene that happens nearly every day in every city all over the world. Colleagues are at the bar, celebrating. Everyone's letting their hair down a bit—relieved, laughing, and having a good time. Why? Because they just finished a big project. Maybe it was a new product launch or a new marketing campaign, or maybe the team just delivered a proposal or presentation. You can almost see the stress lifting as they ease into the satisfaction of a task completed. It feels good. There's a sense of accomplishment and of bonding, having come out the other side of the effort unscathed. But if we went around the table and asked each of the players what result, exactly, they were celebrating, what would they say? Was *finishing* the result they were after? Was the project a success? Why did the project matter to begin with? What goal did they accomplish beyond it just *being done*?

In my experience, most people celebrating at that table can't answer those questions. I've been there many times before, savoring a drink and a sense of completion, while also wondering if and why our work mattered. When we celebrate a launch, we rarely (if ever) actually know if the launch is successful or not. It takes days, weeks, or even months to gather the actual data, and by then, we've normally moved on to the next thing.

The very sad truth is that *most businesses don't sufficiently define goals*. Even fewer titrate those goals to the core desires of their business. Sure, at some level, high up in the tower, there are targets for sales, revenue, profit margin, and stock prices. But what about that campaign I worked on? That redesign? My team? My job?

Between 2012 and 2019, while at Clearhead, we were engaged with over one hundred Fortune 1000 businesses. I probably spoke to another two or three hundred about their needs. Amazingly, I can count on two hands the number of companies that had clearly defined, comprehensive goals. And I can count on one hand the number of businesses that made the effort to then translate those goals down to the levels of teams, projects, and employees. All of those in that tiny subset were native digital, direct to consumer businesses or software companies. The rest of them, including some of the most famous and best-loved brands in the world, were either vague, resistant, or silent when it came to articulation of goals.

Twenty or thirty years ago, before the analytics revolution, this would not have surprised me. Most everything was driven by gut, measured by effort or charisma, and tracked simply to determine completion. The results and their relative significance simply came out in the wash. *People knew if they were being rewarded—through validation and compensation. But very few people knew if their work was good, "great," worse, or meaningless.* But that was then. By 2012, I presumed that we'd refined the way we set and measured goals. We had not. I was shocked how many great companies and executives skipped over goal setting. Sometimes, they cut corners. Sometimes, they just "yadda yadda-ed" it, suggesting that the goals were obvious or insisting that they were somebody else's responsibility. But mostly, they'd revert to a single, blunt metric or two and stop there. Sales and conversion rate. Revenue and margin. Clicks and likes.

But are those really the only goals? Do those goals effectively measure the overall health of a business? Do they measure the entire value of a project? Of a team? An employee? What happens when our work is not measured and tracked back to goals? What happens when we are unsure what the goals even are or why they are what they are?

Whatever industry you're in, you're probably familiar with what happens next. Without well-defined, understood, and properly tracked goals, alignment breaks down. Teams fracture. Silos get established. Malaise sets in. Employees persist not out of a sense of value or purpose but out of necessity or social pressure. Increasingly, they don't persist at all. They just leave. The single largest motivator of employee happiness and retention is a correlation between their work and why their work matters.

And that correlation matters to me—as an entrepreneur, but more importantly, as a person. Along with a safe work environment and equitable treatment and compensation, I believe that *goal definition is an inalienable right of every employee*. It's what allows us to understand if and why our work matters. To understand why it was or was not achieved. That is something that every employee should have access to. It assumes a lot of us. It assumes that our goals are motivated by and linked to our desires. And it assumes that we have the capacity and commitment to goal setting. Is that really *so* much?

Apparently, sometimes it is. Early on at Clearhead, we were hired by a beloved luxury fashion brand to optimize the user experience on their website. This particular website was the source of nearly a billion dollars of annual revenue. So it wasn't just a website—it was functionally their flagship store. Over time, we began to focus on the product detail page, where we uncovered several obstacles that, upon testing and redesign, yielded significant benefit. The percentage itself was modest—something like 3 or 4 percent—but for a massive brand doing so much volume and wherein each transaction can be thousands of dollars, the prospective gains added up to a massive figure.

Our client, the director of user experience design, was so pleased with the outcome that she set up a meeting with the creative director, who held a lot of sway at the brand—hardly unusual for a fashion company. Shortly thereafter, we proudly marched in with our data and our story, expecting high fives or thumbs-ups. However, we got nothing of the sort. The creative director balked from the outset, saying that our work was not "good design." After the initial shock and defensiveness, we discovered the CD did not care about the conversion rate. It did not matter that their customers preferred it or that the new design would make the brand more money. Her goals were not conversion rate or sales or average order value. But she couldn't actually articulate what her alternative goals were. Her lack of clarity nearly sunk our contract.

This experience confirmed for me the need for a holistic view of goals—a perspective which, in this case, understood brand *and* experience *and* revenue. What I thought was obvious, what had been so consistent and singular for most of our other clients—that "good design" was the design that we could prove worked for the customer and for the bottom line—clearly needed better definition for our clients. Without a more balanced definition, I was certain we—and any other companies they worked with—would continue to fail. And so I became *very* interested in getting *very* specific about goals.

What Are Goals, *Really*?

We have a lot of names for goals—targets, objectives, aims, intentions, etc. Increasingly in the SaaS world, the common term is *OKRs* (Objectives and Key Results). Whatever you call them, naming goals assumes describing a qualitative objective, or desired outcome, and pairing it with a quantifiable metric. *It's taking the notion of success—however you and your business's desires have come to define it—and clarifying the point at which you can tell if you've achieved it or not.* Without goals, we float aimlessly in a sea of work, activity, and projects without ever recognizing the value beyond something being "completed" or "launched." If desires are the generative force and purpose for doing something, goals provide the shape, size, and location of that force and purpose.

There's an overused, but certainly true, saying that goes something like, "If it's worth doing, it's worth measuring." Goals are what help us distinguish between work worth doing and everything else. They give us something to aim toward. They allow us to reflect on previous baselines and performance. And they help us determine when we have strayed from our targets and need to double down, pivot, reconsider, or panic.

Whether we call them OKRs or not, *a goal as I define it includes a qualitative statement of objective alongside a SMART goal that, necessarily, includes a KPI* (Key Performance Indicator). If, for example, you owned a chain of fitness clubs and you wanted to define a goal related to member loyalty, it might look something like this:

Objective: Industry-leading customer loyalty.

SMART Goal: Achieve 90 percent annual membership retention rate for fiscal year 2023.

Together, those two statements comprise the company's member loyalty goal. Of course, *that single goal does not make up an entire scorecard.* As with desires, goals have multiple dimensions. Additionally, there are enterprise goals, department goals, employee goals, project goals, and design goals.

To be clear, my understanding of goals has been hard earned. Early in my career, I was guilty of many of the same behaviors I described above. When we formed Clearhead, I still viewed goals as mostly blunt and binary concepts. Coming from Insound, I could only see sales and retention, revenue and margin, or conversion rates and average order values. And so I was not totally surprised when our clients at Clearhead indicated that all they cared about was either sales or order conversion rate, or that they struggled to even quantify their targets. For a moment, the simplicity of these goals worked. They seemed to help define success both for our experience design work and for our engagements. But very quickly, we saw the limitations of such a narrow view. At Clearhead, I recognized that sales and revenue were not especially valuable if they could not be retained or if they were not profitable. Similarly, I understood that we could not operate efficiently or sustainably if we did not develop and retain our employees.

You get the point: there was no single goal. Success wasn't just about hitting home runs. We needed to pitch well, play good defense, and attract, retain, and develop the best players. To define winning, we needed more than a single metric. We needed a balanced scorecard.

The same was true for our clients. Whether we were talking about their entire business or a specific product or experience we were designing with them, success could only be evaluated holistically. After all, you can improve conversion rates simply by putting products on extreme sale (which most retailers do, all the time, at their own peril). To improve margin, you can just make things more cheaply. To acquire users, you can overspend on advertising. Individually, each goal only tells part of the story. Together, however, you can get a picture of overall health.

Why Goals?

We articulate goals—whether for a company, a design, or an individual—for a couple of very good reasons: to define a desired outcome and to determine a way to measure our progress toward it. No single goal, however, can provide a complete picture of the desired outcome or the relative performance in pursuit of it. A company cannot be evaluated exclusively on the basis of sales, which are blind to costs, efficiency, innovation, loyalty, and satisfaction. Similarly, a design cannot be evaluated strictly by clicks or conversions, which are blind to the intentions behind them.

Seems obvious enough, right? And yet, *most businesses under-define goals*, if they define them at all. It's no wonder, really. One reason is that we often think that defining goals requires us to do the hard work of developing alignment among disparate groups and disparate goals within matrixed organizations. But here's the thing. Goals don't get voted on. They are not democratic. If desires are personal, or monarchic, then goals are autocratic. They are inscribed by leadership in service of desires. They are logical to the point of being imperative.

Some goals also remain under-defined because of the perceived challenges inherent in tracking and measuring goals. But this isn't necessarily true either. *Goal tracking is not nearly as challenging as it was just a few years ago.* We live in a digital age in which all sorts of research, tracking, and analytics tools have removed or mitigated the challenges.

Nevertheless, many leaders still don't understand the extent to which goals truly matter—how a well-defined goal can help orient a team around their efforts and provide a measuring stick to assess progress. I have a friend who once met Red Auerbach, the former general manager and coach of the Boston Celtics who helped guide the franchise to unprecedented dominance. Upon meeting the sports legend, she asked, very earnestly, to what he attributed the team's success. According to her telling, Auerbach drew a series of arrows on a piece of paper, all pointing toward the center. The implication was clear—*everyone in the organization was on the same page about what success meant and how to achieve it.*

The story offers a great description of what separates the best institutions from everyone else. As with the Celtics, at Google, Amazon, and Apple goals are clearly defined and rigorously measured. Goals tell the players on the court where to go, what to do next, and most importantly, why they're doing what they're doing. Without quantifiable goals, every game would be chaos. And without clear goals, a business—and its employees—will struggle for evidence that they're achieving good work. If you never know if what you're doing matters beyond simply earning a paycheck, what motivation do you have to keep doing it?

With clear goals, you can also define restraints. When they're specific and bound by time, goals keep you on a path that avoids risk and desire drift. Across a business, clear goals create a clarity of vision and a team alignment that engenders efficiency and ingenuity.

And so if goals are essential for growth, "leader led," and easier to track than ever before, then what's the problem? If it's not the complexity or the effort required, what's the issue? Well, maybe most institutions don't know where to start. Or rather, where to listen.

Listening for Our Goals

Ideally, businesses are *always* listening for goals. They are tracking and measuring performance to see how they are doing (in relation to goals). More frequently, however, the listening is periodic. Companies spend the time before the beginning of each year, and then sometimes again before each new month or quarter, reflecting on the prior period's performance and listening to determine how they should define goals for the next period. And while the scorecards are not always balanced and goals may not always be defined top to bottom, front to back, the infrastructure is already in place for listening for the definition of goals and listening for the measurement of performance.

As for the former—goal definition—*it starts where we last ended: desires.* So dust off that last pentagon you worked on, wherein you defined five dimensions of institutional desire (Intrinsic, Functional, Social, Developmental, and Experiential) and ask yourself, "How will I know if these desires are being fulfilled?" or "What will indicate to me that our outcomes are matching our desires?"

The aim is first to develop enterprise goals for the whole organization. Enterprise goals are the small set of desired outcomes that gets addressed by the most senior leadership team, at the company's most significant moments (town halls, quarterly business reviews, annual reports, etc.). They are the rubric for determining the overall health of the business. They are the goals to which the CEO is most accountable.

All goals, and especially enterprise goals, should track back to those desires we defined in the previous chapter. The more granular goals should naturally flow down from the top. And while I happen to have a special place in my heart for those granular goals that motivate individuals, for the purposes of this book, we'll be talking mostly about the goals that measure the growth of institutions and the products or services that they design. To this end, there are functionally two sorts of goals we'll be concerning ourselves with: front-of-house goals (those that relate to the performance of customer-facing products and services) and back-of-house goals (those that relate to internal functions, processes, and operations).

Unlike desires, however, goals are not inscribed by founders or chief executives alone. Instead, they should absolutely be *defined* by the leaders responsible for the business functions that correlate to each dimension—with input from outside forces and factors. For example, the CMO should be responsible for goals that track back to Social desires, the CRO or CFO should be responsible for goals related to Developmental desires, the COO or CPO (chief people officer) should tackle Experiential desires, etc. They should listen to those desires, in concert with previous performance and signals from the market and from the CEO. Based on what they hear, they should then define and organize the institution's goals around these five dimensions:

1. **Product:** These goals align with the Intrinsic desires for a business. Every business provides either a product or a service or some permutation of the two. So goals here are

meant to define whether the product or service is cogent. Is there evidence of product-market fit? Metrics related to customer satisfaction, product adoption, or engagement are appropriate here.

2. **Customers:** These goals align with the Functional desires of a business. Whereas Product goals speak to utility, Customer goals reflect the felt benefits (beyond satisfaction) of the product or service. These goals relate to loyalty, passion, and evangelism. How do customers feel about you and your product? Do they love you? Do they want to come back? Do they like it enough to tell other people about it?

3. **Market:** These goals align with a business's Social desires— namely, marketing and sales. Are you effective at creating demand and moving customers down the funnel from interest to purchase to retention? How effective are you at generating demand and converting it?

4. **Financial:** These goals are aligned with the Developmental desires of the business. However, Financial goals are beyond just top line and bottom line. They're connected to the unit economics and the cost to serve. Are your cost of goods (or services) in line? Is there risk to long-term financial sustainability?

5. **People:** These goals are aligned with a business's Experiential desires: the experience of employees, the overall working culture the organization creates, and the policies and processes that make up the company's environment. What is it like to work inside the organization? Is it a place they want to stay? Is it inspiring? Is it efficient? Is it equitable?

Each goal should be defined and then added to create a third pentagon.

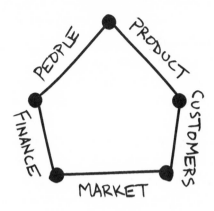

These five dimensions both directly relate to the institutional desires of a business and, *taken together, comprise a balanced scorecard for the institution.* Every desire has unintended consequences. Similarly, every goal can have either a positive or negative effect on other important goals. However, by connecting our goals back to institutional desires, we ensure a through line to mission, vision, and values, as well as to the entrepreneur's more personal desires.

Aim for at least one goal for each dimension (though occasionally a dimension may require more than one enterprise goal) articulated by the responsible leader and approved (or revised) by the CEO, who is ultimately accountable for "the enterprise."

Each goal should be accompanied by an objective and SMART goal, as we've already discussed.

A Financial goal might look like this:

#radically-improve-profitability

Increase EBITDA margins by 50 percent in 2023 over 2022 final results.

A Customer goal might look like this:

#solve-the-churn

Reduce customer churn rate by 25 percent, or to 12 percent of all subscribers, in 2023.

Though the above might seem plainly obvious, *it's important to note that they each contain an objective, a target, a metric, and a time horizon.* This precision is intentional. I've seen too many businesses fall short of the detail necessary for goal setting. They wind up with goals that are too vague or metrics that aren't the best indicators. Or they learn, too late, that the target is either not realistic enough or not ambitious enough.

Perhaps the most common misstep I've seen, though, is businesses substituting tactics for goals. For example, a business might say that their goal is to hire fifty people during the year or to launch their new product on time. Those are tactics with binary outcomes. They may, in fact, be the most critical tactics for the company. But they are not the ends that you are aiming for. *Those tactics are in pursuit of something else—a better product, more sales, more efficiency, less employee churn.* Let tactical goals be set at the project or department level. Make sure enterprise goals really describe the ends you desire and how you will measure against them.

Once approved, listen for priorities among those goals. Run the same thought experiment we covered with Desires: if you had $100 to spend in pursuit of these goals, how would you spend it? Ask the leadership team the same. What do you hear? I've found that the answers can help inform how to prioritize the time and effort spent on problems, which we'll tackle in the next chapter. But for now, just ask and listen.

Suffice it to say, there is more available software and skills related to performance measurement in the market today than ever before. Digital analytics practices exploded onto the scene in the early 2000s, around the onset of Omniture and Google Analytics. And that was only the beginning. Today, we have marketing analysts, product and experience analysts, financial analysts, A/B testing analysts, and many other roles at our startups—all designed to listen to the available data and give us a sense for how we are performing.

Historically, analysts have been overused and misused by organizations. They are exploited as on-demand report administrators.

They're the smart people who get us the data we need to prove a point. They're trained in the software that most of us only barely know how to use. They can create models and data arrays and functions and queries. But they are also scarce and valuable resources. To listen properly for performance, this role has to be streamlined. The analytics departments I've been able to help build have had three ostensible functions: (1) to understand problems most worth solving, (2) to validate hypotheses that we are testing, and (3) to measure performance against defined goals. Almost every other request is a distraction. However, most requests can (and should) get rationalized around those three functions. For the purpose of this chapter, my point is that we listen for performance by asking ourselves (or the analysts and researchers who support us) whether or not we are achieving our goals.

I could probably write chapters upon chapters about measurement and analytics and how businesses can better organize around those practices. But this isn't *that* book, and there are many other, more qualified authors who've already tackled those subjects. For much further reading, check out the appendix, wherein I've listed a handful of books about measurement and analytics that I can confidently recommend.

Aligning Goals

By now you have three pentagons—one for entrepreneurial desires, one for institutional desires, and one for goals. Line those up again, with those personal desires as the biggest shape on the outside, the startup desires within that, and the goals inset as the center bullseyes. *Turn them so the dimensions are aligned and listen in.* Do they nest nicely? Is there friction? Do you hear squeaking? There is no science to this. You are simply looking to see if there is a logical through line between desires and goals. Are you expecting a level of work effort from your people that will betray the experiential desires of the company? Are you attempting to penetrate a market that is not described in the startup's Social desires? If there is friction in these answers, then you are at risk of going off course. Your goals may be pointing away from your mission and vision. Or they may be pulling you apart from your personal desires. In either case, your goals should *not* compromise the purpose of your institution or what you require for personal fulfillment. They should align.

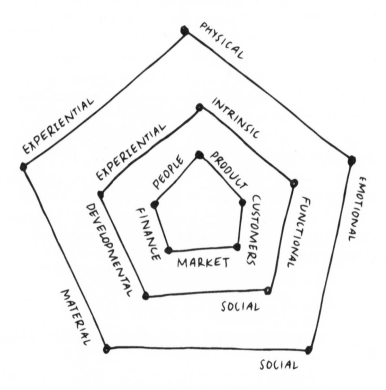

As you align these pentagons, there is no single right way to share your codified goals throughout your organization. I tend to be an oversharer in these regards. Before a new fiscal year begins, I like to kick off annual planning by introducing enterprise goals, explaining how we arrived at them and how we will measure them. At that point, we would additionally share department level goals, which were crafted by department heads in direct response to the enterprise goals. Collectively, we would describe how the parent goals (enterprise) had birthed the child goals (department) and how all pointed back to the mission, vision, and values of the business (the proxy for desires). And with that, we would challenge more junior managers and employees to follow suit for projects and career development and performance goals.

These goals were included as headers in leadership planning documents and agendas. Everyone could see the assumptions we were always operating under and directing ourselves toward. But you can—and we did—take goals further. We embedded them in everything we did. We created tasks in our task management tools that would require all projects to begin with the review of higher-level goals and, if necessary, the articulation of project-level goals. No work could begin without appropriate goals for the simplest of reasons: without goals, there was no way to indicate if our work was good, not good, great, or awful.

The effective propagation of goals, however, requires more than just the loud voices of leadership and the forced compliance of task management software. It requires practice and repetition. And so as a founder, I began every town hall meeting (which we held every other month) with a presentation of our balanced scorecard. We would re-share our goals and visualize our performance with a simple green, yellow, or red indication to provide the team with a general sense for how we were progressing. From there, we'd get more specific around how we were performing vis-à-vis each metric, what evidence we had gathered, and what problems we saw standing in our way.

Department and project-level meetings followed suit. During annual planning, and throughout the year as new initiatives arose, goals were defined and approved only when they were properly formed and abiding by the direction of enterprise goals. With this system in place, the entire team at Clearhead could effectively communicate the goals of their work and how they related to the larger goals of a project, a department or—of course—the entire institution. When I say "alignment," that's what I mean.

Though I'm not a chiropractor, I like the word and implication of that term: alignment. It's about setting the core structure of an organism into place so that it can proceed in the world, free of aches and pains. The same is true for business. Alignment can feel inconvenient. It requires time and money. And it's not a one-time thing. But when there is a clear picture of what alignment looks like and a process for doing it and repeating it, the entrepreneur, their institution, and their people can grow confidently, with balance but without the fear of strain or breaks.

And as soon as we are sufficiently aligned, we can start doing that heavy lifting of taking on our problems, which are, in fact, the fulcrum of GPS and really, this entire book.

chapter 7

Problems

In the fall of 2014, Clearhead was two years old and growing rapidly. Around that time, three separate circumstances led us to one of the core revelations that inspired this book. First, our growth required operational challenges—hiring people, changing org charts, improving communication, and letting go of some things. Though on the surface Clearhead was bright and shiny, I feared that some of our systems might be breaking down. Second, we'd begun to hit a wall in our pursuit of more design "wins." We had more talent, more hypotheses, and more trusting clients than ever before. We had two years of testing and learning on a scale I never could have predicted. And yet, most of our experiments were not winning. Finally, we'd just started working with a new client who was more trusting of our work than any of our previous clients. With a bigger budget and freer range to work on any part of their digital experience, we were going to be tested like never before.

That client was Vitamix—the premium blender company. From the get-go, they bought into our value proposition and our methodology. To them, we really were the "hypothesis validation company."

They were excited about Lean principles and A/B testing, and they desperately wanted to improve their e-commerce experience and business. After a couple of months of mutual admiration, however, they posed a challenge: they wanted us to redesign how the "filters and facets" worked on their website. The team at Vitamix was certain that they had a design problem. If we could design some clever, elegant way to sort products, they were confident customers would get to what they wanted faster and would be much more likely to add products to their cart.

Though our teams had many specific design hypotheses, the prevailing ones seemed to portend a product comparison feature that allowed you to select multiple blenders and compare them through a single screen or view. We listened carefully to the client and researched how other companies addressed this sort of solution. We initially felt satisfied we had done our due diligence, but as we got deeper into the hypothesis development and design process, we tensed up. The budget for this experiment was significant, and we knew that our reputation with the client was on the line. In fact, some of our faith in ourselves was on the line. And so, before we went any further, we decided to pause and take stock. Our team ran more remote usability tests and spoke directly to more customers. And in that moment of pause, we learned the single most important lesson about healthy growth.

It was Ryan who put that lesson into words:

"Matty," he said, *"the problem is that we didn't understand the actual problem!* We thought the solution was about filter and facet design. But the more we listened to customers, the more we realized that they don't even understand the facets. They don't think in terms of motor power, speed, and blade angles. The product comparisons are almost meaningless to them. They don't need a blender comparison tool; they need help recommending the right product based on simpler things that they do understand—price, size, color, etc. They need a 'blender recommender!'"

What Ryan was suggesting was so obvious and yet so counter to how we had been working. It also unmistakably related to the pain I was feeling about our growth as a business and our flatline winning percentage. It wasn't just Vitamax. We'd been skipping over problems in most of our experiments. But the ones that won seemed to be the ones *where we first really defined the obstacle, and the hypothesis was mapped directly back to it.* And the opposite is true! When we didn't solve problems or when our work created new problems, value was neutered or destroyed.

Ryan imagined every business, every product, and every experience as a set of problems standing between the business's desired outcome and the end user's needs and actions. Picture a stack of problems piling up on the desks of your startup. Ryan reasoned that the more our design work reduced that stack of problems, the more key metrics grew. And the more that stack of problems festered or grew, the more growth receded. In this new light, we could see that *it was problem resolution rather than hypothesis testing that was the actual source of growth.*

I knew Ryan was right as soon as he presented this idea. In my mind, *The Lean Startup* had never fully accounted for the cost and opportunity cost of testing and failing. Back then, Lean seemed to presuppose that capital was always available and that, if you failed with one idea or one product or—heck—one startup, you could just try another one. Lean put a premium on the hypotheses, the experiments, and the speed of learning. But it did not seem to account for the Theory of Constraints, which focuses on the most critical obstacles or limitations that hinder a system's capacity to succeed. The more Ryan and I talked, the more we heard an obvious bridge between the two methodologies.

Over the coming months, we put our new understanding to the test as we designed and tested our "blender recommender" and— voilà—it was a big, statistical winner. We'd solved more problems than we'd created. That was a big win, but the bigger win was that through Ryan's insight, we gained a new perspective on *everything* from our design thinking to our operations.

Typically, when businesses identify their goals, they quickly shift into action. The floodgates of ideas open: I have a project! I've been wanting to do this! Let's get a budget approved and get people on it! Almost every business I've ever worked with operates this way. And then, at some point, they finish and move on to the next thing. Maybe there's a report or a postmortem. Maybe there's even an experiment. But rarely does the business discern why their project worked or did not.

In that long leap between goals and ideas, there are a lot of slippery banana peels. And by moving so fast, leaning in when they should take a moment to lean out, businesses are skipping an essential step in the process. They may indeed achieve a goal, or several goals, but have they solved the actual problem? In my experience, most new things create some value for some people and create problems for others. It's the ratio between those results that ultimately determines growth.

What Are Problems, *Really*?

Even more so than "desires," "problems" have a reputation problem. In business, they imply complaints, defects, impasses, and the opposite of progress and action. Problems are things to be avoided. But in reality—and in GPS—problems are simply the inverse of a solution hypothesis. In fact, rather than thinking of a problem as the underside of a solution, I find it helpful to think of the solution hypothesis as the underside of a problem. Imagine trying to test a vaccine without fully understanding the virus. The same is true in design and in operations. The problem is what presupposes the solution, not vice versa.

Bear in mind that when I use the term "problem," I am speaking broadly. I am not limiting the discussion to problems related to customer-facing products, services, or experiences, or to the internal operations and performance of a startup. Problems can relate to marketing, to supply chain, or to people. They can be defects, bugs, obstacles, or impasses. *But they can also be unmet opportunities. If you have a tremendous asset that you are not fully utilizing, that is, in fact, a problem.*

Whatever its nature, truly, there is a lot to love about problems. Unlike solution hypotheses, problems are quantifiable. They exist in the present. They can be measured, dissected, and fully understood. And fortunately, we have more tools and talent focused on the capture and understanding of problems than ever before.

It is also far easier to get alignment around problems in a business than it is to build consensus around the solution. That may seem counterintuitive, but I see it happen all the time. People are entitled to their opinions. We all have biases and pet projects, which is why solution brainstorming tends to lead to debate, factions, and compromise. Problems are less speculative. They are meritocratic— earning their place in a hierarchy of problems. And if we listen, they come bearing evidence.

Whereas desires and goals provide a startup with purpose and momentum, problems provide it with constraints and leverage. They focus us and help us release our grip on ideas and opinions. They allow us to collectively lean back into the obstacle, knowing that the solution begins with a hypothesis that, until it is validated, is mostly supposition.

The trick is *getting to the roots of the problems* and then *to the problems most worth solving.* And this requires a good deal of excavation and prioritization. Every startup is riddled with problems, but *growth comes in proportion to the relative value of the problems you choose to solve.* If you were a homeowner who had an outdated bathroom but also a busted water main, you *could* certainly redecorate your bathroom, but old wallpaper is not the problem most worth solving; the broken pipe is. In design and in business, you have to look past the symptoms and the solutions to find the root problems.

To do this, you must first recognize that a future solution is not the same thing as a problem. That's not always as obvious as it sounds. At Clearhead, most of our clients would say things like "We need to redesign our checkout" or "We need to personalize our website," as though those broad solution hypotheses were, in fact, problems. It's a little like a doctor prescribing a treatment plan for an illness before diagnosing the illness itself. It doesn't make sense to operate this way.

To distill down to the root we have to ask a series of whys. Why is it not personalized? Why does checkout need to be redesigned? Eventually, when there is no logical answer to the question "why," we arrive at the root problem.

For example, "not personalized enough" could mean that loyal customers of women's clothing are frustrated that men's shirts and pants are consistently prioritized in your global navigation and site-wide promotions. They know your brand and products, and they expect *you* to know *them* better. "Not personalized enough" could indicate that a person who always signs in to checkout does not need to be prompted with the option to check out as a guest. Or vice versa. In other words, rarely do the problems require wholesale changes. And, in fact, without sufficient understanding, our shiny, new ideas tend to create more problems than they solve.

Why Problems?

Following our success with Vitamix, we redesigned our entire delivery process with an emphasis on problem understanding and prioritization. Whereas we had previously sprinted ahead into hypothesis testing following goal definition, we now leaned back. The change didn't come naturally. Sprinters build a particular set of muscles and prioritize the speed of reaction. Our muscles had been built disproportionately around hypotheses and experiments, and our speed to testing was a core value proposition.

As we started to reconceive how we worked and how we sold our services, however, we began to use our muscles in a whole new way. We were no longer sprinting. Instead, it felt more like riding a bicycle, where we had to keep one wheel spinning hypotheses and another spinning problems in order to move forward. These "wheels" worked together and allowed us to cover more ground than we ever could have in short sprints. Everything we were doing at Clearhead—and functionally everything that all successful start-ups do—was about understanding the problems most worth solving and testing the hypotheses most likely to succeed vis-à-vis those problems.

Nearly as soon as we changed our thinking around UX and product design, we also began to look at our internal operations. If problem solving was the fulcrum of growth for design, we thought, wouldn't it follow that it would be the key to institutional growth as well? Why not run Clearhead as a business dedicated to constantly addressing our own problems most worth solving?

We homed in on our *"Capital P" problems* (a nickname we gave to the truly elite, highest order or magnitude problems most worth solving—the ones that demanded leadership's vigilant attention), and we returned with a whale of a problem: we were an agency that made money by selling service hours. As you'll recall from Chapter 4, we were initially optimized for "chargeability"—the number of billable hours that we worked divided by the total number of hours worked. And that meant that every non-billable hour—time spent on sales, marketing, HR, or innovation—was perceived as pure cost. Our billable target, as a company, was between 65 and 70 percent. *Those* were the hours we needed to be solving problems for our clients. In order for us to grow profitably, we needed to hit those numbers.

But what of the rest? The underside of the problem, in this case, became our solution hypothesis. We ultimately believed that Clearhead would achieve healthy growth if we dedicated the other 30 to

35 percent of our work hours to the problems most worth solving. Whereas before employees could come to me with an idea and justify an investment based on their belief in their hypothesis—after all, it was only an experiment—there was now a crucial step to take in between goals and solutions: researching and identifying the problems most worth solving. At the leadership level, we did this in relation to our enterprise goals. Department heads did the same for their practices, and employees did the same for their accounts and their careers.

Within a matter of months, we went from being the "hypothesis validation company" to the company that solved problems through research and experimentation. It required an extra step. It required more explanation. But our diligence paid off. Once we got going, the results were indisputable.

Not only did we sustain triple-digit growth, not only did our clients begin to win more and solve bigger problems, but the new constraints to GPS created additional alignment and better collaboration. What we discovered rather quickly was that centering on hypotheses had been divisive. Everyone wanted to test their idea. People were also possessive around solutions. They poked holes in others' solutions, questioning why they focused on one segment versus another or why they expected 3 percent lift versus 5 percent. Focusing on problems, on the other hand, was unifying.

Problem data was frequently less disputable, as it was based on known obstacles. Additionally, we all experienced a certain catharsis through the effort to get from symptoms to root to problems most worth solving. By the end of a GPS session, people seemed to be willing to disabuse themselves of biases and pet projects. They'd been cleansed and were united by a purpose—to solve those Capital P's.

We also found that the best hypotheses were almost always the mirror image of well-articulated problems. They showed us what to do or not to do. If something was making customers unhappy, stop doing it. If we found a major, unmet need, try meeting that need. If there was friction in the process, remove it. In time, we realized that the greatest solutions were not born from genius or inspiration so much as they came from our love of the problem.

The Theory of Constraints purports that there is really one root problem underlying any product, service, or system. In GPS, we found that our best hypotheses focused on a single, known, and significant problem rather than many smaller, superficial ones. The former approach frequently yielded positive statistical difference and few unintended consequences while the latter left our "batting average" flat. *So rather than trying to solve many small problems, we went goal by goal to identify the singular problems most worth solving.* At any given time, rather than attempt to whack dozens of moles, we would work on two or three Capital P's. This was true for institutional problems as well as design problems.

As we began seeing increasing benefits of GPS internally, new interest was arising from our clients externally. Once we explained the rationale and the process, I was amazed at how quickly our clients took to it. I noticed a leap in the trust and investments that our clients made in us. When we would compete against traditional digital design agencies for business, our pitch was simple: You could either hire the fancy, award-winning, big-name agency that will show you beautiful work with no proven benefits. Or you could hire us—the smaller, less fancy, more methodical agency that quantifies problems, tests solutions, and can show you precisely to what extent our work succeeded. GPS was a godsend for our service and our operations. But it was also a nifty sales tool.

Listening for Problems

Twenty years ago, we could barely "hear" anything. But today, we have web analytics, app analytics, network analytics, and marketing analytics. We have digital survey tools, voice of customer tools, remote user testing tools, heatmapping tools, tree testing tools, and card sorting tools. We have natural language processing tools, machine learning, client side A/B testing, server side A/B testing, and tools that use algorithms to learn and optimize. There are so many ways for us to gather signals for problems. Most of you are likely aware of them, and most of you probably use them or rely on them to validate assumptions.

We use various applications to confirm something or to report out, defend a decision, or justify an idea. But rarely do we use this incredible set of powers to simply listen for problems. And even if we do, when problems get gnarlier, people tend to cover their ears. If the problem seems unsolvable, we don't want to hear about it.

Imagine how much smarter and more likely to grow we would be if we could harness the talent of the fast-growing research and analytics community and apply as much of their capacity on problem understanding as we do on solution validation. Imagine that. Now imagine if it wasn't just the researchers and analysts. Imagine it was your whole startup. Imagine it was you, the entrepreneur. Wouldn't you feel more confident in your ability to grow and scale in a healthy way? I know I would.

So with myriad tools and too much data, how do we tune in? I'm glad you asked, because this is perhaps the most critical moment in GPS. Problem identification necessarily defines what you will hypothesize and test. The road to healthy growth doesn't begin here, but problems do compel action. And so, with a sea of signals and noise, where do we point our ears? We go goal by goal, of course. We look at each of the goals (or OKRs) on our balanced scorecard, and we ask ourselves: "Why might we not achieve this goal?" "What stands in our way?"

This first round of questions is like shaking trees—lots of small problems and symptoms begin to fall from the leaves. Listen closely, consider each item, and then ask the "five whys" (or two or three or however many it takes). Keep listening and, as you get closer to the root, ask yourself the following:

- What goal does this problem obstruct?
- Who does this problem impact?
- When and where does it impact them?
- How widespread is the problem?
- How severe is the problem?
- What evidence do we have that the problem is real?

Ask those questions for every goal and every problem. Eventually, they'll lead to your root. At the same time, patterns will emerge. What those patterns usually show is that one root problem consists of many of those smaller problems, symptoms, defects, and obstacles that fell off the tree when you first shook it.

For each goal, there may be several root problems because each goal depends on multiple systems for success. The inverse can also be true. Over time, you might discover that the root problem for one goal is the same as the root for another goal. And that, as Martha Stewart used to say, is a very good thing. Because that means that the team can align and collaborate on solutions with different solution hypotheses for a single purpose that can impact more than one goal.

As you make your way through the practice, you will find that some problems are redundant and some are related to or dependent upon others. Within those roots, problem clusters or "themes" will emerge. A problem theme is the nexus of several related root problems that impact many systems and users. Because of their disproportionate impact, in GPS we prioritize by themes, precisely because they are the sum of multiple roots and many smaller problems. Additionally, by the time we arrive at these themes, we have significant insight into their constituent parts, who they impact, when and where they impact those people, and why.

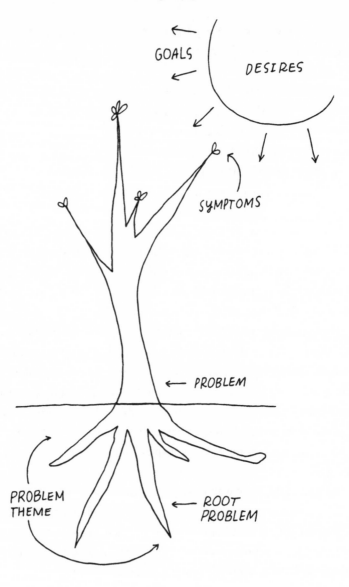

As with goals and desires, I like to give problem themes hashtag titles. They could be things like "#slow-to-hire" or "#search-irrelevance" or "#checkout-friction." Whatever the case, I like to follow the hashtag with a one sentence description of the root, and then I like to tag all of the subproblems with the hashtag that they relate to, making it easily searchable and indexable.

As you begin to organize your problem themes, you will use data and evidence to substantiate your claims and to size the problem themes. When you've exhausted the discussion—when you've leveraged your research, analytics, and anecdotal information and listened to each other and your sources—it's time to seize the prize. To do this, ask, listen, and answer these questions:

- How widespread is the problem?
- How severe is the problem?
- How much evidence is there that the problem actually obstructs the goal?
- What is the cost of solving it?
- What is the cost of not solving it?

As you continue to work through this practice, you'll see some themes wherein the evidence is strong but the benefit of solving may be limited. You might see other themes wherein the benefit is massive but so is the cost. In any case, if you listen closely, you'll begin to hear alignment. Lesser problems will be de-prioritized. Some problems that seem promising will be rejected for lack of evidence and will require more research before they are acted upon.

At Clearhead, we created derived metrics to score our problems based on the aforementioned criteria (size of problem, severity of problem, evidence that it is real, cost to solve, cost to not solve). However, even without a method for scoring, prioritization came naturally. We knew that we could not solve every problem. We knew that not all problems were most worth solving. But when we observed our tree, with desires and goals at the top and problems below, it inevitably became clear which were our Capital P's and which were the smaller P's. The Capital P's, of course, became the focus of our efforts. But we necessarily created some space for smaller, easy fixes, as well as what we called "Just Do Its"—problems that were either so simple to resolve or so urgent that we could not wait for another research and prioritization cycle.

Ideally, this practice leads to identifying the problems most worth solving in the right order. Of course, in startup world, few things actually pan out "ideally." When businesses trip up in this stage of GPS, I find that the mistakes tend to fall into one of these common problem "traps":

- The problem is not closely connected to a goal
- The problem is actually a solution masquerading as a problem
- The problem is not at the root level—it's actually several (possibly conflicting) problems rolled into one

And to be completely honest, there will be moments when you have to set aside some rigor just to get something done. You may get pressure from investors or the market, for example, that is so urgent you just need to get all hands on deck to address the crisis. In those moments, you'll have to reallocate the capacity and resources you would normally give to GPS, until the crisis has passed.

Adapting to urgent needs this way doesn't mean you have to skip problem definition altogether. Keep listening. Give it a good faith effort and know that any insights you glean will pay off later. You will have reduced your problem stack, moving more files to the "solved" side, with every move.

The single biggest risk in problem identification is skipping this step altogether. Jump from goals into solutions at your own peril. It's a massive chasm in between, and it's the leap that dooms most businesses. Problems are the bridge between those two steps. They're invaluable constraints *and* the source DNA for winning hypotheses. The most successful living entrepreneurs—Bill Gates, Jeff Bezos,

Elon Musk—talk constantly about solving massive problems. While you certainly don't need to follow their lead, you should absolutely listen.

Once you have your problems clarified, though, I have great news. It's time to start up. We've leaned out and tuned in. And now we can start to press ahead—accelerate even—into solution hypotheses, experiments, and ultimately, outcomes. We can do this confidently knowing that we've set up the parameters and requirements for growth. So while our teams may never do *exactly* what we would do in the way that we would do it, we can be assured that they will share the same purpose, that they are pointed in a common direction, and that they remain focused on the problems most worth solving.

chapter 8

Hypotheses

Before Amazon was Amazon, before we had SaaS for content management and commerce, and before we had Google Analytics and Optimizely the web was a mess. Without sufficient baselines, targets, or standards, websites would change fundamentally and unpredictably all the time. Home pages were constantly thrown out and reconstituted. Product pages were tweaked and turned. And checkout—don't even get me started. There were single-page checkouts and seven-page checkouts. There were guest-only check-outs and members-only versions. Everybody was trying everything, and nobody knew if any of it was working.

After many years, a couple of startups, and who knows how many failed experiments later, I had made marked progress in founding Clearhead. Nevertheless, I still had a ways to go. During those first couple of years at Clearhead, we did two sorts of experiments: the simple "let's see what happens if we change a color or a call to action" variety and the "let's change the entire home page or—heck—even checkout" sort. The former was fairly straightforward to execute, while the latter was far more difficult and speculative. But in both cases, the hardest part was getting our clients to clearly articulate their hypotheses. What did they believe would be true if we made these changes? And how would they know, specifically, that the change was successful? Everyone loved their ideas and their design comps and the increased ease with which they could test A versus B. But the actual work of articulating the hypotheses? Not so much.

Over time, we made progress. In spite of the lingering effects of seventh-grade science PTSD, most clients began to embrace the effort and rewards of being "Lean-er." But I also noticed a disturbing trend: the work that UX, product design, and optimization teams were doing was being bifurcated from the work that visual design, brand design, and marketing teams were doing. As a result, the biggest departments within our clients, those who had most of the budget and sway, were still driven by big ideas, campaigns, and instincts.

Push came to shove frequently. And in those early years, our work got pushed and shoved right out of the way all the time—perhaps no more clearly than during our time working with Keurig. Back then, Keurig hired us to take on a sliver of design work that was being rigorously tested. That excluded everything else. And "everything else" took precedence. Our efforts were paused so the "real creatives" could do their work. In anticipation of new models of higher-end coffee makers, they decided to...all together now...fully...redesign...the website.

The brief for the redesign—as it was repeatedly communicated to me—was to "make coffee beautiful." One sentence. Three words. No explicit subject. And yet, in those three words, there were hundreds of unstated hypotheses. Hypotheses that would never be formally tested. Hypotheses that had no clear target or baseline. I knew that what Keurig really wanted was a website that was more usable, enjoyable, and likely to drive more sales, especially of these new makers they were introducing. But the leap from "make coffee beautiful" to a more usable, enjoyable, higher-converting website was a massive one.

Unsurprisingly, Keurig did not successfully land the jump. To their significant credit, however, they reached back out to us within days of their relaunch. Together, we worked to reverse engineer their redesign efforts into a series of smaller, more discrete, testable hypotheses. In a remarkably short period of time, we optimized their way back to something that was more usable, enjoyable, and sufficiently converting. As to whether the coffee appeared more beautiful, I never did find out.

What Are Hypotheses, *Really*?

If it is true that everything we do in business is fundamentally an experiment, it follows that, *underlying everything we do in business, there are hypotheses*. At their core, hypotheses are ideas, rendered naked of hubris, restated as specific claims of change, including their benefits and success metrics. They help you answer these key questions:

1. What do you believe to be true?
2. How will you know whether it's true?

Seems simple enough, right? Yet, wherever you've worked and in whatever roles, it's likely this is not how decisions get made. Decision-making more often looks like this: people in power or with perceived charisma convince others that certain initiatives require funding. Their ideas are approved and advanced through some combination of intuition and experience. Most of the time, the first "evidence" that the initiative has succeeded or failed comes only when the product or service hits the general market. Some companies do product testing during development, but the big test is usually getting a product into people's hands and seeing if they like it. In fact, many businesses don't even think of that milestone as a test. They think of it simply as the "launch" or "release."

By that time, it's too late to course correct in any meaningful way, and you're back to sitting in a room where the next charismatic individual prevails and sets into motion a new set of ideas that beget new (relatively untested) launches.

Hypotheses are kryptonite to the charismatic model. A hypothesis is only useful if you can prove that it is either valid or valuable. They are the sober, humble foil to "ideas." In Lean Startup, they are the atoms of what we Build, before we Measure and Learn. They are the germs of "MVPs" (minimum viable products). They are the prerequisites for experiments. They are all of those things. And, in GPS, they are the bridge between the problems most worth solving and the outcomes. They are what prevent us from slipping on the banana peels of ideas and leaping into an abyss.

In my experience, the best hypotheses—the most valuable ones—tend to share some common traits. A well-formed hypothesis makes an unambiguous "change claim." It describes what you believe will happen, based on a proposed change, that is different from what is happening now. It will also articulate how you will know, with confidence, that your change claim is valid. Our prompts at Clearhead used the following structure:

"I believe that..." (describe the change and what you expect to happen as a result of it)

"If I am right, then..." (state the benefit *in terms of a specific metric*, its difference from the control, and the level of confidence you require)

From the previous chapter, you will recall that, at Clearhead, we were briefly chasing the wrong problem and solution hypothesis for Vitamix and their blenders. The weak hypothesis began something like this: "I think we should redesign how users compare blenders on our website." Fortunately, we did not try to test on that. Instead, after a great deal of research and refinement, we arrived at a much more valuable hypothesis: "I believe that if we create a blender recommender tool that takes simpler, intuitive inputs from new users and provides product recommendations based on those inputs, prospective customers will better understand which products are the right ones for them. If I am right, I expect to see a 10 percent improvement, with greater than 95 percent confidence interval, in the add-to-cart rate for new site visitors."

A quick note on improvement targets and confidence intervals. The former should be realistic (in my experience, high double-digit gains are rare and triple digits are miraculous) but also bold enough to justify the cost of the effort and the likelihood of some regression to a mean. As for confidence intervals, the industry seems to have settled into targets of 95 percent or better. If you are interested in learning more about either subject, I'd recommend you check out some of the books that I reference in the appendix, many of which address experiment design and statistics.

Our "blender recommender" hypothesis was valuable on many levels—it was well-articulated, targeted, and measurable. But my favorite thing about it was that it gave us a clear place to start. In other words, *if a designer, an engineer, and an analyst read this hypothesis, they could likely begin to sketch out next steps.*

Let me also confirm something that might seem obvious but is critical to restate: not all hypotheses relate to design, features, or products. In fact, most hypotheses relate to business operations and changes that are not, specifically, digital. Changes to compensation are born from hypotheses. Same with promotions. And benefits. And software selection. And office location. You get the point.

For example, many companies today are wrestling with how to support flexible, remote work environments while also engendering a workplace culture and collaboration. In light of the COVID-19 pandemic, some have moved to completely remote models, others have begun to compel a "return to the office," and most seem comfortable living in a hybrid middle ground.

Underlying these decisions are surely many assumptions—some spoken, some implicit. But I suspect very few of them are formally tested. So instead of simply hoping that a virtual workplace will be more attractive for new applicants and instead of assuming that a return to the office will lead to greater productivity, what if we actually articulated a hypothesis and then attempted to validate it? How about: "I believe that if we institute a three-day in-office and two-day remote or optional work week, employees will feel the combination of workplace culture and flexibility that they desire. If I am right, we will see a 20 percent increase in employee job satisfaction among employees with tenure of one or more years, when compared to last year and as measured by our annual employee climate survey." Just like the hypothesis for the Vitamix "Blender Recommender," this version for improving employee happiness (and hopefully retention) begins with a clear change claim and a means of validation. True, it does not contemplate a controlled A/B test. But it is, nevertheless, a well-formed hypothesis.

Why Hypotheses?

Hypotheses matter not just as a tool for validating progress but as a tool for modeling transparency for your employees. By now, you've heard my contention that employees have an inalienable right to know if and why their work is good or not. *Hypotheses are what help us frame the pursuit of those answers.* They can serve as the means for validating whether their personal performance is sufficient and if the work they are making is solving problems and meeting standards.

Beneath the righteousness of hypothesis testing, there is a more fundamental question: why do we work? Nobody works simply to "do stuff." Aside from money, what motivates people in their work? In my experience, answers are relatively simple: we either work to (1) solve some set of problems, (2) achieve success, or (3) avoid failure. The problems we solve through work may be virtuous, or they may be very pragmatic. Success may be institutional success in pursuit of company goals, or it may be a sense of personal achievement or advancement. And we work to avoid failure—either the shame of not measuring up or the discomfort of not making progress. Regardless of the motivation, it is hypotheses that help us define whether our work is valid, in the terms that we define it. We want to know if our work...works.

Hypothesis-driven startups—specifically those that employ GPS—also create better leverage for their founders. Lean startups do not expect or require their founders to be the singular agents of the best ideas. On the contrary, they distribute that responsibility outward, toward the greater team and the market itself. Similarly, *companies that fundamentally embrace evidence-based design—in their product and their operations—engender cultures of curiosity and meritocracy.* They help their people ask and answer that big question: why do I work? In fact, they demand that their people ask and answer it. In this way, employees become as responsible for their own fulfillment as their employers. As a founder, I cannot describe the relief I have felt over the years in realizing that my job is not to be "right" but rather to create the conditions that allow us to understand what success means and what problems we need to solve to achieve it. Along with continuous problem research, hypothesis testing becomes the defining activity for a healthy, growing startup.

And yet, we often fail to approach hypotheses with the respect they deserve. The reality is, if businesses were laboratories, most would be full of cheap ideas, sloppy conditions, and insufficient rigor. Gus Fring from *Breaking Bad* would scoff at the lack of hygiene in most businesses. And he'd be right. We get lazy. We overreach. We pile up banana peels. And when we don't articulate clear hypotheses, we introduce other variables without even thinking about them. As a result, we get inconclusive evidence, unintended consequences, or negative side effects. And we don't know why.

But the startups that grow—healthily and disproportionately— are the ones who are constantly testing and learning from the hypotheses that consider the problems most worth solving.

Listening for Hypotheses

In a way, you've got a head start on listening for hypotheses since you've already practiced listening for problems. *Listening for hypotheses is tightly linked to listening for problems.* Without that fundamental titration, the hypothesis is likely to lead to unintended consequences, including net new problems, wasted resources, or the opportunity cost that mounts as we allow more important problems to fester. The most successful hypotheses, in contrast, are almost always the underside of a well-articulated problem. For example, if you know that your business is doing something to turn users away, the best hypothesis begins by considering what would happen if you stopped doing that thing. Similarly, if there is something that your users want that you are not sufficiently providing, the best hypothesis would test what would happen if you provided that feature, product, or benefit.

Remember, GPS is built on the premise that growth is correlated to our ability to listen to and then resolve our problems most worth solving. We've made it this far—to the hypothesis development phase. So let's not stray from our problems now. Our solution hypotheses most worth testing have necessarily listened to those problems most worth solving.

At the same time, as we tune in to problems most worth solving, we also need to open our ears to a broad range of sources for hypotheses. *The inspiration for a good hypothesis can come from anywhere.* They can come from an intern or a random customer just as easily as they can come from the top. The source of many of the most successful hypotheses we tested were not defined by the CEO or even by a lead designer or engineer. They were born through unbiased, less mechanized thinking.

That's why, although I do not value the quantity of hypotheses over their quality, I do recommend listening to the wisdom of the crowd. *Whereas desires and goals are autocratic—they come from the top—and whereas problems are meritocratic—they are based on evidence—hypotheses are democratic.*

And so, listen liberally to hypotheses. The higher you are in the organization, the more I suggest you loosen your grip on hypothesis development. Not that you should shirk that responsibility. It's more that you should disabuse yourself of the assumption that you have (or should have) the best hypothesis.

Generally speaking, you listen for hypotheses in the same places you've been listening for problems. Customers or prospects will provide the basic ingredients for hypotheses through customer service, surveys, or user tests. Even when the data is anonymous and purely quantitative—as it frequently is with digital analytics data— we can listen to where people are trying to get to and what stands in their way. We can read product reviews to hear what people like and do not like. We can look at previous A/B tests or experiments and see which variations worked for which segments and against which metrics. We can look to competitors or market leaders to see how and why they do what they do. They may have struggled with problems similar to yours. How did they resolve that issue of navigation? How did they resolve this issue of hiring people? All of these can be transformed into an "I believe" statement with an "if I'm right" metric attached.

Finally, make sure you listen to the memory of your institution. Whether it is through long-tenured employees or those who've previously researched and tested similar hypotheses, the walls of your startup can talk. The loss of institutional knowledge, especially in an era of high employee turnover, can be massive and costly. For this reason, I am a proponent of institutional learning libraries. These can be as simple as databases of generic solution hypotheses assigned to common problem sets, alongside links to any company deliverables related to said problems or solutions. They can be searchable, indexable folders containing previous research and findings, organized by product, UX, client, or time period. Or they can involve SaaS that is designed for product, customer, or employee feedback, adapted so that it has containers for problems, hypotheses, and results.

In combing through the bounty of evidence, we can begin to cobble together hypotheses that are precise in that they address known problems or unmet opportunities. As we listen, we should also be sure to seek clarity on what our hypotheses have to offer our problems. We often like to get cute with hypotheses—preferring the novel to the obvious. But I have found that the most successful hypotheses are evident once you start listening for them. Here are some starting points:

- What problems do you expect to solve?
- Are those the problems most worth solving?
- How will you know if the hypothesis is valid?
- What could the cost be to test the hypothesis?
- What could the benefit be if the hypothesis is valid?
- What will you do based on the findings?

Conversely, try to avoid those nefarious "hypothesis traps" that undermine our efforts to address the problems most worth solving, including:

- It's not closely connected to a problem most worth solving
- It's not specific enough for employees to begin work on
- It's too broad and is actually several hypotheses rolled into one
- It is based on the assumption that because it worked for others, it will work for you
- It has the wrong metric assigned for validation

To avoid these traps, *develop hypotheses that are honest and specific about what they believe and why they believe it to be true.* Hypotheses are, by definition, speculative, but they should be informed by a known problem as well as a clear idea about what goal they expect to impact.

Similarly, avoid hypotheses that are vague or the sum set of many smaller, discreet hypotheses. The risks of "ganging" disparate hypotheses are manifold. Because of their complexity, they are more likely to confuse designers, engineers, and analysts, each of whom might interpret the implicit assumptions differently. Further, they are harder to measure. Finally, the more change we pack into a single hypothesis, the more likely we are to create unintended consequences.

You'll know that you've fallen into one of these traps if your experiments are getting harder and harder to design or if the results are consistently inconclusive or, worse, up for debate. If you find that you're stuck, simply circle back to the beginning of this chapter and start again. Remember: the best hypotheses draw a straight line back to the problem. The worst ones amount to a pile of banana peels, just waiting for us to trip on them.

Prioritizing Hypotheses

There are lots of possible hypotheses for every problem, but based on time and resources, only a subset are testable. So you're probably wondering where to start.

Before we get to that, let me say the most obvious thing about hypotheses: *they are hypothetical.* We do not know if they are valid or how the change will actually impact something. If we did, we would not need to test anything. Thus, it's often more useful to begin by deciding where not to start. To be specific, if the hypothesis is *not* aligned clearly to a problem most worth solving, it should not be tested. Until the problem is understood and the connection to the solution is convincing, it should be put on the shelf. Similarly, if the results are predetermined, it should *not* be prioritized for testing. By this I mean that if the organization is going to proceed with a change regardless of the results of an experiment, it's best to proceed with production and analysis and leave bandwidth for hypotheses where the outcomes and rationale are genuinely uncertain. In limited amounts, there is no shame in this. No company has infinite resources, and time comes for all of us. Occasionally, in the interest of time or cost, you just need to move forward with an idea, while still acknowledging the underlying goal, problem, and hypotheses. You should still measure the change, even if the confidence of your insights is not the same as during a controlled experiment. The bigger waste would be spending the time and money to test something with no earnest intent to learn or optimize.

With those hypotheses out of the way, where do you turn next? Sometimes you just have to start where you are, with the things that have already been decided and funded. Maybe you have inherited a road map or set of preexisting priorities and find yourself in medias res. You'll need to continue in that direction until you come to a natural point of re-prioritization.

At Clearhead, this happened all the time. It was often not feasible to rewrite a road map on day one! Our clients had their plans made for the quarter, if not the year. We expected as much, and we spent time defining desires and goals and, most importantly, researching problems most worth solving. Simultaneously, we reverse engineered their road map into a series of testable hypotheses. In almost every case, once we had defined the problems, usually within ninety days, the client would ask us to reset their road map based on how their hypotheses aligned to Capital P's.

Obviously, most of you reading this are not running an experience optimization agency similar to Clearhead. It is far more likely that you are running your own startup or overseeing a product, design, or department. In any of those cases, the previous scenario still holds relevance. You have probably already either created or inherited a road map, and the shift required to be more hypothesis-driven will necessitate the definition of desires, goals, and problems. Do not fear. Keep calm. Continue with business as usual as you begin your GPS practice. Once you get through problems most worth solving, you can effectively re-prioritize your road map based on new hypotheses that directly address those problems.

As for how our clients eventually prioritized those new, problem-centric hypotheses—for most, the process involved worksheets. Lots of worksheets. Many of them included some formula for predicting the lift of an experiment based on segment size, traffic, and the purported benefit contemplated by the hypothesis. I am not a fan of using this method as the key indicator of priorities for the simple reason that all of those inputs are so speculative, but especially because of the assumed "lift." I completely support the exercise of contemplating potential benefit and determining what improvement would be commensurate with the change and effectively validating. But when it comes to prioritization, *I prefer a score or derived metric that accounts for the following*:

- Alignment to problem
- Confidence in validity
- Cost to test
- Potential benefit

I use a simple, unscientific linear scale for each of the inputs. One to five or one to ten. And as you might expect at this point, I also weigh the "alignment to problem" disproportionately in the final calculations. So, for example, let's imagine that you are the head of e-commerce for a sneaker company, considering two potential hypotheses. One is based on a competitor's case study and hypothesizes that by adding 360-degree product videos on product detail pages, they will achieve a dramatic increase in add-to-cart rates. In this case, you do not have evidence that their current product detail page photos are actually a problem—all you have is a presentation that was shared by their competitor at a conference. On the other hand, PDPs do receive a lot of traffic, and the logic of the case study was compelling.

Now, let's suppose that you know for a fact that 10 percent of customers are abandoning their carts early in checkout to search for discounts on third-party coupon sites and never returning. And let's suppose that your team has its own hypothesis about suppressing the coupon field until the final stage of checkout, rather than the first page. In this example, the alignment to a known problem would likely supersede the allure of the (hypothetical) potential benefit.

This is not the only way to set priorities, but it is a version that highly values well-understood problems. Remember, as is always the case with GPS, we are practicing a series of adaptable poses—there is no "best." But once we've found those hypotheses that closely connect to the problems most worth solving, we're ready for the fun stuff. We've done our research. The lab is clean. It's time to roll up our sleeves, get out the beakers, and begin experimenting.

chapter 9

Experiments

In 2013, I gave a series of talks called "Test Everything." Six years later, I was traveling the same conference circuit, talking about how conversion rate optimization can actually hurt your business. What happened in between to shift my perspective? Well, everything really.

For one thing, I did not believe the idea that every experiment was a de facto winner, that the learning gained from every test carried intrinsic value and justified the risk. It just wasn't true. At the same time, I began to notice a second, more insidious trend: all forms of experimentation and validation were becoming subsumed by A/B testing. Things had changed since the times when A/B testing software was relatively niche and prohibitively expensive. Now it was not only massively popular, it was widely accessible. In the frenzy, many businesses either forgot about or devalued every other form of design and product testing. The conventional wisdom at the time said there was only one "best" way to test and that was via an A/B test. This wasn't just semantics. To me, these behaviors were becoming a real issue.

There were those words: *test* and *everything*. Did we really mean to test everything just because we could? Every piece of content? Every design? Every feature? Every product? Every service? I was convinced that every business decision was, fundamentally, an experiment. But was I equally convinced that *everything should be tested*? The answer was a firm "yes, but..." Not every change can or should be A/B tested. But everything can and should be tested and validated.

This distinction is important because, even now, when A/B testing is easier than ever before, it still requires valuable time and resources. Not every problem warrants that investment. Nevertheless, for over a decade now, businesses have been spending huge sums of time and money A/B testing anything they could. Even startups, for whom opportunity costs are disproportionately high, operate this way—the very opposite of Lean. On some level, we've clearly lost the thread.

We can get it back. We need to, because the goal is not to A/B test everything, but rather *to understand the extent to which we are actually solving problems*. And now that we've done all this work in GPS to arrive at this moment—wherein the hypotheses are inextricably linked to the problems most worth solving, which are themselves linked to goals and desires—let's not get distracted. Let's stop testing for testing's sake and experiment in a way that actually solves those problems.

What Are Experiments, *Really*?

We use the word "experiment" in GPS—rather than "test" or "validate"—because "experiment" is a word that assumes a hypothesis and rigorous procedure. It also suggests curiosity and the opportunity of genuine discovery. It is uncertain on some level but focused on finding meaning. It is both open and attuned. It is a lot like listening itself.

But we have to open our ears to all kinds of experiments, not just those things that we A/B test. There are dozens, if not hundreds or even thousands, of things we are experimenting on every day where we are looking for clarity, even if it is not a 95 percent confidence interval. We just don't call them experiments. We call them projects, inventions, decisions, initiatives, tactics, and plans. Every new idea that gets introduced and pursued in business qualifies as an experiment.

Through gradual experimentation, I came to see that growth was correlated to the resolution of problems most worth solving, and if many of those problems were internal or operational in nature, it logically followed that I needed to experiment beyond the digital realm. That I needed to turn my ear inward, listen to and experiment upon the business itself.

In other words, experimentation isn't just about "front-of-the-house" (i.e., customer-facing) choices. It's everything in the back of the house as well. Every time you hire a new employee, you're conducting a whole bunch of experiments. Are they the right fit for the position? Are you paying them the right salary? Every time your business reaches out to a prospect to sell something, that's an experiment. Are they the right target? Is your pricing structure a fit for them?

At Clearhead, we were as intentional about experimenting on ourselves as we were in our customer-facing UX and product design work. We used the same language for testing designs and features on websites that we used for business decisions. Whether we were creating a new line of Clearhead branded swag for marketing, holding a company retreat, or amending employee benefits, we walked through the steps of GPS. We articulated desires, aligned goals, defined problems, created hypotheses, and then moved into experimentation.

In these instances, we used either surveys or anecdotal observations as a means to validate our hypotheses. No, they weren't

A/B tests, but rest assured, there were hypotheses, problems, and goals. And there was an expectation that evidence would be rigorously captured and presented back to the company to describe what we had learned and why we were confident (or not) about future outcomes.

Because everything in GPS is conceived of as an experiment, it is essential to remain very open to the wide swath of validation methods. So don't forget about your usability tests, surveys, regression tests, pre/post-analyses, and the other less quantitative, but still useful, ways of making determinations and supporting decisions. After all, our desired outcome is not "more A/B tests" or "more data" or even "more statistical confidence." It's healthier growth through greater understanding.

Why Experiments?

Experiments are where the rubber meets the road. They are the moments wherein our ideas either get exposed for their shortcomings and unintended consequences or validated for the extent to which they actually solve problems. This is where we leave the comps, the wire frames, and the hypotheticals behind, and we see how actual users—prospects, customers, or employees—respond to a change. Experiments are our feedback loops. They can turn hope into confidence. But they can also humble us, reminding us that our opinions are not smarter than the sum of our audience.

For the people at our startups, experiments are also highly rewarding. When we experiment, we shift our poses. Whereas we previously spent so much time leaning back out, listening for and trying to understand our problems, when we experiment, we are tuned in, confident, and agile. Moreover, we are designing things, building things, and making changes. Experiments may not always be "validating," but they should be "gratifying" in that they leave the realm of the theoretical and enter the realm of the actual. Was our design any good? Did this new process improve things? Do people like the product? When we experiment, we get answers to those questions. We also get closer to our customers.

Through experiments, which followed hypotheses, which came after problems, goals, and desires, Clearhead raised the bar on everything. We got better at listening and learning. Our hive mind grew stronger. And because experiments provided that active, inventive outlet, we retained employees at an unbelievable rate. Our steadfast commitment to experimentation and all that it implies—meritocracy, transparency, curiosity—was, in my mind, the single greatest contributor to both our financial success and our employee happiness. As we used to say at Clearhead: Experimentation is not a thing that you do. It is *how* you do things.

But this was not always the case. Before GPS, I frequently saw—and sometimes was party to—experiments wherein the hypothesis was not connected to any known problem. Clients would choose to spend time and money changing colors or moving images around, simply because they could. Other times, the metrics within an experiment failed to address the hypothesis. For instance, if the problem was a lack of product or brand information clarity, a company might develop a hypothesis that directly addressed said problem. But if the company chose the wrong primary metric, such as order conversion rate, for the experiment, they were unlikely to get a meaningful answer. That's the true value of finely tuned experiments. The system breaks down if you don't align the measurement with the actual problem being solved and the hypothesis being tested.

Remember—we don't experiment to "win" or to "sell more." We experiment to determine the extent to which our hypothesis is valid: whether it is sufficiently solving a problem. Growth, in turn, follows the problem solving. Whether your experiment is top of funnel or bottom, whether it's front of house or back, whether it's an A/B test or some other modality, GPS helps ensure a degree of logic and rigor that mitigates the disarray of "test everything." It's the practice that helps startups graduate from "testing things" to a culture of experimentation in pursuit of the problems we must solve and the outcomes we most desire.

Listening for Experiments

Experiments always start with the formulation of a plan. When we talk about the "rigor" of experimentation, a plan is assumed even in the most minimal scenarios. Without it, there are no assumptions or procedures to follow. It's not a practice—it's just flailing. Ideally, that experiment plan will consider every step of the GPS process, alongside the practical details required for implementation. Generally, these are the ten most important questions to ask as we move into experiment planning:

1. What are we actually trying to learn through this experiment?
2. How can we best achieve that learning—what method of experimentation will we be employing?
3. How long are we willing to wait to make a determination—what is the amount of time or data that we are willing to wait for before there is some risk to the experiment?
4. What resources are we willing to spend on the experiment—what is the cost we are willing to pay to learn if our hypothesis is valid?
5. Do we know what problem we are trying to solve—is it a problem that is most worth solving?
6. Do we have a clearly stated hypothesis—what is our "change claim" and, given it, is our projected outcome reasonable?
7. What evidence do we need to gather—what information do we have access to and how will it be gathered?

8. What is the best indicator of success or failure—what is the key performance indicator, supporting metrics, and level of confidence we will need to monitor for?

9. If our hypothesis proves to be invalid or inconclusive, what will we do next—are we open to and prepared for failure, including the sharing of insights gained?

10. If our hypothesis proves to be valid or if the experiment is successful, what will we do next—are we prepared for success, including a more permanent change and the sharing of insights gained?

While this is probably not the same approach or rigor a pharmaceuticals company is going to take when trialing a new drug, it's a pretty good place to start for companies simply trying to grow in a healthy manner. It's also something we've tested and optimized through GPS, homing in on the intersection of conscientious and practical.

In order to effectively listen to your experiments, you must first understand how to tune the rigor and fidelity of your plan. If you have written that experiment plan and addressed those ten aforementioned questions, then you know precisely where to look and listen. Do not search for validation where there is none. Do not convince yourself that your hypothesis is valid simply because your experiment did no harm. Or because you already spent a bunch of money going down this road. Instead, trust the plan. Answer the questions your plan raised.

And be patient. We have a tendency to get excited about the outcome as soon as we initiate a test. Mere hours into an A/B test—after all the work to launch the experiment—we long for statistical significance even though we are days or weeks from our desired confidence interval. We get a couple of users tested or survey responses, and we quickly look for any indications of success. The urge toward rapid cognitive closure is incredibly strong. Resist. Whether you are the experiment's designer or simply an interested party, the key to listening is remembering that your plan is your guide. Stick with your plan and your practice, rather than your (excitable) guts.

Planning can also calm most nerves. At Clearhead, we did not have to question the end point or the indication of the results because they were clearly defined in our plans. Impatience could be strong, but we always had a response at the ready. Any time the urge toward rapid closure cropped up, we could confidently say, "We have collected this much of the sample necessary, and based on current trends, we believe we will have a sufficient data set in this many hours, days, or weeks." That's part of what separated an experiment from any old test or the pull of confirmation bias.

We need to hear the answers our experiments return clearly, even (especially) when we don't get the answers we want. However, *you get to decide what to do with the answers you do get.* If your new design didn't move the needle on your key metric, but you found that customers felt it was more likable or easier to understand, make the call that is right for your business. It is always acceptable to proceed with a new idea, in spite of no KPI improvement, simply because it has some other perceived benefit and limited risk or cost. No harm, no foul. But it is far less righteous to proceed without truthfully resolving the questions posed in your experiment plan. In other words, don't pretend that the new design was actually a winner or that your hypothesis was valid if, in fact, it was not.

For those of you who are especially interested in the science (and art) of experiment design or statistical methods, I've included a list of excellent reference books in the appendix. They are each highly readable and generally accessible, regardless of your proficiency with the math. Rather than add to that already tall pile of texts, though, let's stay focused on our practice, which is most concerned with the questions that we ask and our capacity to hear the evidence in the answers.

Finally, listening asks us to be vigilant in resisting biases and noise. We've done all this work to get here—to the point where we hopefully observe growth. But even if we can't observe growth, we must still listen. Ask the right questions and be open to what your experiments respond with. Whereas most of GPS is about arriving at the next, best question, experiments are the opportunity for an actual feedback loop. Listen closely—and with a very open mind.

Once you do, you're ready for the last step in GPS—the one that makes it all worthwhile—outcomes.

chapter 10

Outcomes

I am not a fan of reports. Growing up, I never liked book reports. In business, something about the phrase "direct reports" rubbed me the wrong way. And I'm practically allergic to those eye-straining, tab-pushing, formula-busting things that we brandish like weapons in meetings. It's not as though I do not like data or statistics. To the contrary, I am obsessed with numbers and results. It's more that I resent the implication of reports: that they are sufficiently meaningful in their own right. That they are the end of something. That they are the actual outcome.

When I arrived at Warner Music Group in 2007 after selling Insound, it was not very hard to see the disarray of their direct-to-consumer business. The company had hundreds of artists, and seemingly every one used a different set of applications for their website, their store, their fan club, their email marketing, and their social media. It was a mess top to bottom. What seemed tidier, however, was the company's analytics implementation. A small but mighty team of web analysts had recently done the tireless work of defining events and pages, tagging sites, and attempting to normalize data that was anything but normal.

Soon after my start date, I began receiving a massive, weekly report that included information about the direct-to-consumer performance for every band on the roster: site visits, unique visitors, page views, orders, conversion rate, email opens, clicks, etc. Behind the tiny font on the summary page, there were then drill down views for each artist. It was a massive file, emailed to most of the company, every single week. This report was nothing short of a miracle. It was one very bright person's labor of love. It demonstrated an uncanny mastery of the analytics platforms, some Excel sorcery, and hours and hours of sweat. People talked about it in biblical terms.

And yet, *I had a nagging suspicion that it was all a waste of time.* Without baselines and targets, how could anyone know if the data indicated success, failure, or something in the middle? Without goals, how could they observe problems? Without hypotheses, how would anyone determine if their new products or campaigns were valid or successful?

Moreover, I wondered if anyone *really* cared. Or if they knew how to care about this sort of thing. That was when we decided to stop reporting and see what happened. Instead of emailing out the weekly behemoth, we took a more consultative approach. We worked with the marketing teams to define targets and to look for outliers. We inched our way toward research and experimentation. And something amazing happened. Nobody missed the reports. Nobody asked about them. Nobody complained. Nobody indicated that they were struggling to do their job without them. All of which indicated something that I'd long suspected: reports—unto themselves—aren't worth a whole lot. *Reports are one tiny part of a means to larger ends.* And those ends are what, in GPS, we call "Outcomes."

In fact, those ends are not even "ends," in the strictest sense of the word. In our last chapter, we planned, constructed, launched, observed, and measured our experiments. So it would be reasonable to assume that in this chapter we are at the end of something—that it's time to report, wrap up, and move on. Well, I'm sorry to be the bearer of inconvenient news, but we really haven't come to the end of anything. The conclusion of an experiment is not one finding, one number, one report, or one change. It's a treasure trove of information we can use to move forward with more confidence. *Outcomes are the lit paths on the road to healthy growth. And that path never ends.*

When an experiment is finished, the report and the change (if any) are frequently the easy parts. Or rather, the least complicated parts. You've prepared for this moment in your experiment plans and aligned around desires, goals, problems, and hypotheses along the way. The harder part is the shared learning and ongoing conversation. Why was our hypothesis valid or not? What should we do—not simply right now but moving forward? To what extent did we actually solve the problem? Knowing this, what impact should we expect on our goals moving forward? Did we uncover additional, related hypotheses that we should be testing? Are we getting smarter? Are we growing healthier?

Outcomes are about sustaining learning and improvement. *They're about looking back and striving forward, sharing and circling back.* In other words, outcomes are only barely about the ending at all. They are mostly about the beginning of what comes next.

What Are Outcomes, *Really*?

Outcomes are partially the direct answers to many of the questions posed in the experiment planning we discussed in the previous chapter. They do, of course, require us to document the math and science employed in testing the validity of our hypotheses. A reporting document that shows the research methodology, the math, the assumptions, and the conclusions is absolutely part of the outcome. But they are more than that. Outcomes are everything that happens immediately at the end of the experiment as well as the related activity afterwards, including the conclusions, learning, adoption, and next steps. *Outcomes are the beginning of other, more confident things.* And while that might sound like "more work," it is more informed, more-likely-to-succeed work.

Outcomes begin from the moment that you have collected a sufficient data set for your experiment (according to the plan), but they continue while you address some of the following questions:

1. Was our hypothesis valid?
2. Why or why not—for whom was it valid or invalid?
3. What performance benefits (if any) should we expect to see moving forward?
4. To what extent did we solve the problem assumed by the hypothesis?
5. What new problems might we have either created or uncovered in our experiment?
6. What new hypotheses might we have uncovered in our experiment?
7. What changes (if any) will we be making based on the above information?
8. Should we reconsider our goals or targets based on these outcomes?
9. Would there have been a more efficient way to conduct this experiment?
10. How can we help the company learn from and sustain the benefits of this experiment?

Making better decisions about what to do next is not merely a set of choices between proceeding with the hypothesized approach or reverting to the control. The best decisions don't just answer yes or no; they help you progress by using what you've learned to codify and circulate new problems and hypotheses. Unlike results, which are finite, and reports, which are looking back, *outcomes are always just ahead of you. They are aspirational.* They are what we confidently accelerate toward.

Why Outcomes?

Why do I insist on reframing this step in GPS as continuous motion rather than something finite? Why can't I just chill and celebrate the conclusion of an insightful moment—the culmination of great effort? In part, because *GPS is a practice and not a prescription.* Also, because *growth comes from scale, and scale is not derived through individual insight or success but from the health and wisdom of the hive.* Reports and postmortems tend to overvalue what occurred in the past and whether we did what we said we would do, rather than create momentum for future growth. In both cases, the emphasis is on validation or compliance rather than learning and growth.

Startups frequently use these approaches—reports, readouts, postmortems, call them what you wish—for both front-of-house and back-of-house experiments. Back-of-house experiments tend to be the most opaque. Rarely do they employ control groups or statistics. They are conceived and evaluated in binary terms: Did we do the thing? Did it work? It's not likely that they are ever even acknowledged as experiments at all. Someone ends up making changes to behaviors, policies, operations, and processes, and while data may play into it or be generated as a result of it, context, information, and learning is usually not shared widely. Some survey or cost benefit analysis is circulated among the decision makers. An internal memo—something in the vein of a dry press release—is shared. But employees never actually learn why things have changed. And when things just happen to them, with no transparency, they lose their sense of agency and autonomy.

When these initiatives and shifts in operations are approached as experiments, however, *results are more likely to be shared with the appropriate context and interest in future outcomes.* Can you imagine a scientist conducting an experiment and then sharing the results with a very small group, withholding the impetus and the potential impact, and then just...moving on? That doesn't happen—or at least it shouldn't—and if it did, they would be depriving the world of any broader insight and opportunity for change and growth.

Front-of-house experiments tend to fare a little better. We acknowledge them for what they are. Even if the hypothesis is not clearly stated, they typically involve gathering and analyzing significant amounts of data, and the person who does that is generally tasked with sharing the findings and providing a recommendation for how to proceed. Compared to more operational changes, consumer facing-experiments usually come with the expectation of rigor and transparency.

But how do they respond to that expectation? Most of the time, they simply show the data. They say, "In our test, A did this, B did this, and C did this. Here is the statistical difference we observed and our confidence level and our margin of error." The level of detail and the presentation of the data is intended to cultivate trust. But frequently that trust is challenged by equal, or greater, levels of suspicion.

Most experiment readouts amount to an unimpeachable response to the question of "what?" They also tend to dull the senses and inspire something between boredom and resolution. Certainly these reports are accompanied by assumptions and bullet point notes. But if and when they are discussed, eyes focus on a single point: the winner. Reports, even when they are elegantly designed, train our eyes, ears, and minds to look for certainty.

Inversely, when the experiment does not produce confident statistical difference—when there is no clear winner—people often default to whatever outcome they were hoping for. Instead of searching for deeper, perhaps more complicated answers and outcomes, people will default to the aspirations of their hypothesis.

By that point, confirmation bias and the bias of sunk costs begin to weigh heavily. This behavior, which I've seen repeated endlessly, is not the fault of the report. Reports are both essential and can also be useful and, even, beautiful. But when reports become conflated with "outcomes"—when statistics and the decision of A versus B become the end of the road—*the startup loses more than it gains.*

That report and what it implies might lead to performance gains, but it will rob the institution of deeper learning and better practices. Furthermore, it will soon be buried in a folder in the cloud somewhere, forgotten forever. It will never impart answers to those other, more essential questions. Did we solve the problem? What should we do after we make a change or revert to the control? Why? What future hypotheses emerged as a result of the experiment? Winners are often fleeting. Results tend to regress to a mean.

But learning and optimization are progressive and compounding. I've produced many reports. I've spent hours fidgeting with their design so as to increase their likelihood of adoption. I've consumed exponentially more than I've produced. And yet, whether I was the maker or the consumer, I hardly remember anything I discussed about any of those reports.

This is why we must detach the idea of outcomes from reports. In my mind, outcomes are ultimately the narratives we create—with the benefit of evidence—that resolve the questions from our experiment plan and create momentum for new questions we must consider for the future. I may not remember any of those reports, but I can name shots and lines from all of my favorite movies. And when I hear a good story, every detail, every association, and every inspiration sticks with me. Reports disappear. We hear them briefly, and then they fade. Great stories, however, live on. They change us.

The report is simply a mechanism for providing confidence in those answers. But the decisions we make beyond the binary choices, the information we take away and our capacity to hold and build upon and grow from that knowledge—*those are the more valu-*

able outcomes. Those are the stories that cannot be contained within a report. And they are the stories that we need to tell and that we need to hear.

Listening for Outcomes

So if outcomes are always pointing to the future, just out of reach, but if reports are looking back, taking a snapshot, how do we reconcile the gap? How do we provide the confidence of sound, finite data with the wider aperture and longevity of a thoughtfully written, compelling narrative? It requires the partnership of people in your organization who are quantitatively inclined with those who are more visually inclined, alongside those who are adept at storytelling.

For every experiment we created at Clearhead, we shared a "data story." These were not long-form, text-driven reports nor were they number-driven spreadsheets. *These were slideshow presentations or video with voice-over narration that took the audience through the journey—the story—of one sequence in the GPS process.* They began with goals and traveled through problems, solution hypotheses, experiments, and outcomes. The stories contained ironclad facts, but they also were rich with narrative. They had tension, conflict, plot, subplot, and conclusion. The conflict was the problem. The tension was the hypothesis. The plot was the goals and KPIs. The subplots were the other, supporting metrics that helped explain the motivation and outcomes. The conclusion was the resolution—a succinct distillation of what should be carried forward—both the change and the new insight.

Data stories were co-authored by analysts, researchers, designers, and product managers. Though there were no strict rules on the matter, analysts were accountable for the cogency of the statistics and for additional segmentation, researchers were responsible for qualitative findings and implications, designers were responsible for the data and information visualization, and product managers were responsible for putting the narrative together and articulating it so that others could hear it and respond in kind. Lest you assume that every data story was the length of a novel, they were not. Over time, we developed efficient patterns for structuring these presentations with a focus on their conciseness. We created slides with the fewest words possible. We wanted headlines, charts, and a single idea to allow consumers of the information to listen and see rather than read. We weren't trying to convince anyone of anything or change anyone's mind. We were simply trying to share a story of what had occurred, why it had occurred, and what we believed should occur next.

In preparing the data story, *the team had to listen for outcomes through three different perspectives.* First, they had to consider what facts they needed to listen for to create the data story and how they could hear them clearly and truthfully. To source these answers they referred back to the ten questions from the previous chapter that helped define the "experiment plan," alongside the ten questions in this chapter which helped frame the "outcomes." By asking and answering those questions without bias, they could "hear" the data story taking shape.

Second, the team had to consider the audience and how they would receive the story and the information it included. How could they engender good faith listening? How could they ensure that the key story points were appropriately absorbed? Some of this was accomplished by sharing "assumptions we are operating under" at the outset, in hopes that we could disarm bias and the rush toward closure. And a lot of this was enabled through the information design itself—the data visualization, the information hierarchy, the headlines, and the copywriting.

Finally, the team needed to contemplate how the organization would hear the same story—how the story would propagate and how the benefits could scale. This sort of listening was aided through video recordings with voice-over; through alerts in platforms like Slack, Asana, and Google Docs; and through the conscientious cataloging and indexing of all stories in our shared, cloud-based drive.

At Clearhead, data stories became treasured objects that we valued and referred back to constantly. The art and science of data storytelling became a highly valued skill set in the company. *Data stories were shared internally in small groups, first with the core team responsible for the work, then externally with clients, and then in weekly "all hands" meetings.* Given all of the work that goes into each step of GPS, we wanted to ensure that our data stories were told on every available stage and heard by the widest audience possible.

Whereas reports require a high degree of knowledge and interpretation, data stories assume that the math and science is correct. It's only used as a means to better understand goals, problems, hypotheses, experiments, and outcomes. During data storytelling, nobody was sifting through spreadsheet data. That part was done, and done right, and they knew it. That freed them up to stop looking for loopholes or ammunition and instead opened them up to learning about why what had happened happened and how the business could benefit from it.

Data stories were created for every experiment we conducted, both front of the house and back of the house. They were also how we communicated findings and recommendations to clients. Clients told us again and again how the data stories were highly valued moments of learning—how they took bias and personal motives out of the reporting process. They helped round out the sharp edges of analytics and statistical reports. They gave clients something easily communicable they could take back to their boss—something that could be easily consumed, digested, and reshared.

Even years later, I remember so many of our data stories. I remember the ones about sticky navigation, the ones about inline email forms, and the ones about sales and coupon codes in checkout. I remember the ones about product listing page sorts and filters

and facets. There are more than I can count. But if you tell me the client name and the title of the data story, I bet I can take it from there.

For example, there was that time when one of our clients was testing a new SaaS product that allowed businesses to offer Amazon Prime–like shipping benefits. It was a compelling value proposition, addressing a problem that was increasingly separating Amazon from everyone else. The solution was simple to implement, easy for customers to understand, and at least according to the SaaS provider, promised massive gains. The creators of this product suggested that our client could expect high double- or low triple-digit improvements in order conversion rates.

Like most everyone who'd heard the pitch, we were excited but also a little suspicious. Upon some inspection, we quickly realized the numbers provided were comparing people who selected the shipping benefits in comparison to everyone else. That "everyone else" included people who only visited one page of our client's website and then left. It included the 90-plus percent of visitors who would never check out.

The correlation between the software and the outcome was unmistakable. But the causation was entirely suspect. Their promise was a self-fulfilling prophecy because the people who selected those new benefits were already more likely to convert than most people. To tell the full story of what was going on, we had to listen more openly and more closely. We constructed an A/B test wherein we randomly suppressed the software at the moment it would normally appear. Half of the users who had arrived at certain pages and who would normally get the offer of benefits did not see them. And the other half did. The problem was well understood (lackluster shipping delivery value), the hypothesis was clear (the new service should provide Amazon-like shipping benefits), and we had an experiment to test the change claim.

Suffice it to say, it was a tense situation, rife with potential conflict. The software company did not want to be embarrassed. Inversely, our client didn't want their hopes to be spoiled by data. Our job, as always, was to design the right experiment and listen openly before tuning in to outcomes. And guess what? In a controlled experiment, the results were not as promised. Conversion rate in the variant was directionally positive, but without a high degree of confidence and not nearly to the extent that was promoted. We tested the same software across multiple brands and found similar, but not identical, results.

This was great information to have, but how were we supposed to present it to our client? We were implicating both the sales team from the software company and the people who purchased the software. On the other hand, we were not tasked with justifying a price or a purchase. Our job was to test various ways to employ this new software and to compare those variations to the control. To tell *that* story, we couldn't just deliver a bunch of numbers. We had to revisit the goal, the problem, and the hypothesis. We needed to set aside the overstated claims and the price tag and simply consider the extent to which the problem might be solved and what other outcomes were possible.

Instead of packing everything into a report, we explained our outcomes in a story. We indicated our degree of confidence. And we explained why the results were not clearer or more dramatic. We concluded that by the time the software was serving its offer, customers had already disproportionately made their purchase decision. We hypothesized that by promoting the offer further up in the funnel and through CRM, we could imagine enhanced benefits. Additionally, we surveyed customers who'd used the expedited shipping service and found them to be more satisfied and less likely to contact customer service. And so the software was beneficial. It just was not clearly beneficial in the way that it was advertised or implemented. That was the story we had to tell. And it was far more memorable than any chart or report could muster.

Listening for outcomes requires a lot of us, but most of all it requires that we listen openly and in good faith. When the experiment has concluded, the bias of sunk costs likes to creep in. This particular experiment was rife with potential bias and conflict. However, because we told the story of how we arrived at our conclusions—goals, problems, hypotheses, experiments—rather than simply pointing to the data and our conclusion, everyone involved took the same journey to the best possible outcomes.

Generally speaking, outcomes are defined much less by the discreet changes (or bold ones) than by the capacity of the startup to make continuously better decisions. Winners are fleeting. Problem solving cannot be. Similarly, the desire for cognitive closure is always a risk. When the experiment is done, the urge to move onto the next thing will be strong. But practice patience and openness. Listen before you leap. The problem is not likely fully solved. The goal is not likely exceeded. The story is not fully told yet. That doesn't mean your experiment wasn't valuable—by all means celebrate it. But keep moving through and toward those outcomes. And keep listening for growth.

In GPS we reserve the biggest high fives and the happiest of happy hours not for the completed experiments or the winners but for those moments when we realize that we understand why we conducted the experiment to begin with and why our hypothesis was valid. And like any great practice—whether it's yoga or baseball or painting—*GPS is designed around repetition.* Circular cycles propel our startups forward. Each spin is informed by the previous one. Every advancement is followed by some return. And so, when we come to the end of one "path" in GPS—from desires through outcomes—we must always ask: Have our goals changed? Have our problems changed? What new hypotheses should we test next?

Up Next

We've covered a lot of ground in this part of the book. We started with desires and turned them into goals. We identified the problems that stand between us and our goals. Then we hypothesized solutions and experimented with those hypotheses. Those experiments led to the outcomes that we shared in the story of our findings.

At this point, you should be able to hear things differently than when you started reading. Perhaps you can even imagine building the tracks for GPS at your startup and beginning to steam along toward healthier growth. But *for GPS to truly work, you need more than one set of tracks.* You need your whole team—your whole institution—to learn the practice. They need to be able to then lay down their own set of tracks that lead back to yours. So far, we've talked about a "practice" while moving through a single sequence. Now it's time to build the rest of the infrastructure, so you can expand from the individual to the institutional.

PART III

achieving healthy growth

chapter 11

Putting It All Together

Let's start with the good news: we've now practiced every pose—from beginning to end—from desires through outcomes. By now, I suspect that you're seeing the bigger picture and can, at least intellectually, imagine what is required to practice GPS. At this point, all we have left is to capture the complexities of GPS at the enterprise level.

With so many teams and individuals all striking a different note, how do you find harmony?

When an entire institution is engaging in GPS, people's desires and their goals are all playing the same tune, yet they don't necessarily follow the same rhythm or even use the same instruments. Every team at your startup may be working on a different set of hypotheses and those experiments might only be related in that their problem sets overlap.

Up close, it may sound noisy. But given a broader perspective, it's possible to hear the melody underneath. A company operating with GPS can be like a big band that is expert in the basic tune and has practiced it sufficiently to collectively play jazz with the melody without sacrificing the song. It's awkward at first, as you figure out the chords and rhythm. But the more you practice, the better the whole band gets at it. Once you get the hang of it, each member can improvise while they're supported by the rest of the band. Similarly, in GPS, the steps remain the same on each iteration, but the way each individual and business performs their version of GPS will depend on what you, the conductor, instruct them to listen for in the music.

If you think that sounds difficult, you'd be right. *GPS is not the fastest path to action. Rather, it's the most efficient and repeatable means to healthy growth.* Resistance will be real, and it will be natural, because change is hard. Not everyone likes jazz. Then again, I don't know many people who love the status quo of their startups' present operating system. They may like the excitement of the pace at their startup and the allure of oversized growth, but they equally complain about the chaos and burnout.

Would it be easier to convert people to GPS if it was simply a step-by-step, one-size-fits-all formula? Sure. But GPS is not a formula. It's a practice based on a well-tested set of hypotheses about the physics of healthy growth and tenets that sustain them. GPS is also personal. It holds that your business—and your life—is your own to live and grow in alignment with *your* desires and goals.

Similarly, GPS is not one-and-done. You don't start here and end there. It is cyclical. *It is an ongoing method that continues as long as your business exists.* This doesn't mean the problems you identify will never be solved. It means that as you identify solutions and outcomes, you will also hear new problems and new hypotheses. Your desires will stay true. Your goals will remain clear. But the rest of your practice will advance through a series of cycles that propels you forward until the time comes to reconsider if your speed and direction need reassessment.

For the bulk of this book, you've been learning to play scales and read sheet music. This chapter is about how we put it all together: where the band tunes up, the snare kicks us off, and we finally play the music.

GPS Is Tunable

I've said it before, and I will say it again (and again) in the future: GPS is never perfect. And some of you may be uncomfortable with a model that appears to cede the reins of control to a practice wherein solutions are developed and tested without the explicit approval of the founders. If your goal is complete control or a 100 percent success rate, GPS is not for you. But that also means that growth—particularly healthy growth—is not for you.

Scale requires a high degree of trust and a relinquishing of control. Likewise, growth is iterative and full of obstacles and failure. But rest assured, whether you are a founder, a leader, or simply a curious team member, GPS allows for degrees of control. If nothing else, an entrepreneurial practice must be...practical. Right? In this jazz orchestra, you might not play all the instruments, but if you are in a leadership position, you will get to conduct the band. You might amplify some parts and temper others. You might speed things up or slow things down. But as the keeper of the melody, you ensure that everyone stays in tune with their section in particular and the orchestra in general.

And so while GPS requires a degree of faith in the system, in this section we'll explore some of the ways in which businesses can tune their practices without endangering its basic premise.

Fidelity

Fidelity in GPS is ostensibly the burden of proof we require from our team in the problem research and solution validation. Are we looking for 99.99 percent statistical confidence, or would a highly informed decision based on a survey suffice? As a leader, you can tune the dial on the level of clarity and certainty you expect, depending on your institution's specific constraints.

Some of those constraints will be specific to the type of business you are building. Pharmaceutical companies or banking institutions, for example, demand high fidelity because the risks of error or unintended consequences are so high. Other businesses, and especially early-stage startups, can tolerate more risk and do not have the resources or market data to sufficiently achieve high degrees of statistical confidence. So when we talk about "fidelity" what we really mean is the degree to which you and your startup can tolerate uncertainty and how you value time and money versus risk. To be clear, *evidence must always be collected in GPS*—for tracking goals, researching problems, and experimenting upon hypotheses. But *what sort of evidence you expect and what level of confidence you demand is ultimately up to the founders and their leadership.* It is also something that can evolve as your company grows.

Rigor

We also have the ability—and the responsibility—to define the rigor with which our organization implements GPS. *How, and to what extent, will your business engage in this practice?* For some businesses, it's sufficient to get everyone conversant in GPS, to use it as an internal vernacular or a shorthand for agendas and discussion. Bringing GPS into your organization *could* be as simple as a shift in language—at least initially. For example, getting everyone focused upon and talking about problems most worth solving, rather than on projects and ideas, is a less rigorous shift that can still provide big gains. Meetings could begin with goals and travel through the steps of GPS until they are sufficiently exhausted.

Alternatively, you might be ready for *something more systematic* that can be woven into the fabric of your startup's culture and operations. If so, you can begin to define how GPS provides phase gates for decision-making and approvals and how your work templates and task management systems are designed around the practice. At Clearhead, we created reusable templates and instructions that would allow for anyone on any project—internal or client facing— to spin up a new hypothesis or experiment that would be attached to previously defined problems and goals and would adhere to the fidelity and rigor we expected. There were templates in our task management system, in our working documents, in our shared drive, etc. And these templates came with instructions for use—including how and when approvals were required to proceed. GPS was more than our vernacular. It was the metadata we used to orient ourselves, *and* it was literally how we designed our operations.

Everyone at Clearhead knew exactly how to articulate and propose a hypothesis for testing. Within reason, every data story had the same basic components and was shared through the same channels and progressions. There were even instructions for what to do in an emergency or in cases wherein we needed to fast-track something or break the chain of GPS. This might sound prescriptive, but we found it to ultimately be liberating. It re-centered our work on "The Why" and "The How" in order to guide "The What."

In neither case—the "light" version or the more rigorous one—am I suggesting that everything be written in stone. Businesses change all the time; they have life cycles. *You'll always be reassessing the appropriate fidelity and rigor depending on what will serve your business*, your customers, and your employees the best at the moment. There are always exceptions which can be accounted for at the outset. And there are surprises along the way—some great and some not so. People occasionally need breaks. Sometimes a practice jumps up a level, and sometimes it regresses slightly. But with GPS, the level of rigor is tunable based on where you're at.

Practicing the Steps

With tunability in mind, let's review the steps of our practice. Remember, there is no one right way to do any of these; GPS only requires that your approach consistently be *your approach*. To that end, here's how I've come to think about each of these steps, in terms of their frequency and their function.

- **Desires** should be articulated by founders at the outset of their startup's formation and adapted only as needed and determined by major shifts in direction. Desires can be then translated into Mission, Vision, and Value statements, which can be included in company manuals and on official websites, job postings, and corporate communications. Every time a founder or leader is conducting a "Town Hall" or "All Hands" meeting, I find it useful to reflect back on desires. And while desires can be surfaced through rigorous self-investigation or casual reflection, it is critical that they are honest and clear.
- **Goals** should be defined before the beginning of every new financial year. Minimally, this would include "enterprise goals," but ideally, you turn that dial up to also include department-level goals and individual employee performance goals. Enterprise goals can then be assembled into a "balanced scorecard" which should be reviewed broadly and in the light of day no less than once each quarter. It is critical for the team to understand where the company is under-performing or over-performing and why. Departmental and employee goal updates may be reviewed less frequently, but semi-annually is generally sufficient. Within reason, goals should not change until the next fiscal period.
- **Problems most worth solving** should be codified annually at the outset alongside goals and then, in a more rigorous practice, reviewed at least monthly. While they are unlikely to change at that frequency, they are more fluid and responsive than goals or desires. It takes time to research and understand problems most worth solving and rarely are they quickly solved. I recommend a monthly forum for leadership to review the current research and outcomes, consider whether the problems already identified as most worth solving still deserve that designation, and update where the team is with solution hypotheses and experiments. On the

basis of these meetings, priorities might shift slightly. In truth, though unexpected changes in "Capital P" problems do occur, I've found that problems most worth solving tend to survive for an entire financial year (or longer). Finally, while there is no exact formula for defining how much time to spend on problem definition versus hypothesis development, the entire premise of GPS presupposes that problems are not given short shrift.

- **Solution hypotheses** can be prioritized at the beginning of the year along with goals and problems most worth solving. In reality, though, they are always being articulated and captured, as problems are researched and experiments are conducted. There is no real beginning or end to hypothesis development and prioritization. The startup is always listening for new hypotheses—"shaking the trees" and prioritizing accordingly. Functionally, your annual plan, budget, product road map, etc., is based on those hypotheses that you most want to invest in testing at the beginning of the year. While the budget may not change, the perceived value of your hypotheses might. Prioritization is happening regularly, but iteratively and in accordance with problems and outcomes.

- **Experiments** are constantly running. They are ostensibly your road map of all activities, projects, and programs, set in motion as soon as budgets have been set in place based on goals, problems, and hypotheses. In GPS, every investment in change is considered an experiment and therefore requires an experiment plan. Experiments can run continuously and independently, so long as there are sufficient resources and no conflict in the test samples. Ultimately, experiments are always in one of three life cycle stages: (1) planning, (2) in flight, or (3) concluded and in analysis.

- **Outcomes** should be codified, based on analysis, research, and data stories, and then shared as soon as they are available. Outcomes are always coming out "hot from the kitchen." Frequently, they are shared first with key stakeholders—those who the outcomes most directly impact. From there, the data story should be recorded, indexed, and propagated through wider presentations and alerts as appropriate, and depending on the size and perceived value of the findings and next, best steps.

Every startup has a different level of resources and a unique capacity for investment and risk-taking. In that way, there are myriad ways in which the above steps can be injected into a business's culture and operations. The minimally viable practice, however, accounts for all of these aforementioned steps and defines some baseline for definition, prioritization, and review. The goal is not the "most GPS" or the "perfect practice," so much as it is rightsizing the fidelity and rigor to your startup.

GPS in New Startups

The simplest time to implement GPS is when you're about to launch a new startup or when your startup is in its infancy. If you're prelaunch or premarket, you're likely still deciding how to run business operations. Presumably, the team is small, and your processes are highly adaptable. The slate may not be blank. You may have legacy processes, task management software, and preconceived notions. But the field is still very green. Maybe too green, in fact. You might not even be sure what your goals should look like or how to identify problems when you're so early in the endeavor. Try not to worry. GPS was built for this; it's why we start with desires. *No matter where you are in your startup, you have desires.* You might not have articulated them yet, but you have them. Time to dig into them. Using these desires, you can establish an initial set of goals for your new venture.

Because you are in your early stages, with limited historical data or baselines for your business, and because your team is likely small, a lower fidelity version of GPS is to be expected. Don't aim for perfection. But *as you establish standing agendas, presentation templates, and systems for approvals, endeavor to include SMART goals, problems most worth solving, and solution hypotheses.* Document the definitions of these terms and the assumptions of GPS in a company handbook or FAQ doc. Challenge yourself and your team to practice the vernacular of GPS. Then adjust the fidelity and rigor dials as you progress.

When we started out at Clearhead, we used cultural touchstones to reinforce the practice. Weekly data storytelling presentations were held during lunch and streamed for remote employees. Town halls started with desires and goals and ended with experiments and outcomes. Every other week, the leadership team met to review our problems most worth solving. Employee development plans and reviews conformed to our desires and goals. Everywhere we went, we lived and breathed GPS. Though it was different from any other company we'd previously worked with or for, GPS eventually became completely normal. In time, it seemed impossible to imagine some other way of operating a startup.

GPS in Existing Businesses

Installing GPS practices at a mature startup or legacy business is like building a bridge across a vast river. On one side of the water is the status quo. On the other side is a future of healthy growth, engendered through listening, problem solving, and a robust GPS practice. In the middle, at the moment, all most people can see is the fast-flowing risk.

When you're already up and running and open for business, you have systems in place. You have OKRs. You have agile product teams. You have some prioritization criteria. You conduct research.

You even A/B test things. On the other hand, you might not have clearly heard or stated desires. Your scorecard may not be balanced. Further, you are probably oriented around projects rather than problems. And in all likelihood, you've not thought of operational changes as experiments. Eleven chapters in, however, you know the value of GPS. You want to change. You want to practice. But where and how to start?

First, *always start with the start.* Functionally go through the desires process, rewriting values, missions, etc. If you've not listened for your desires and those of your startup, you may already be off-track for healthy growth. You can go through this exercise without disrupting the operations of your business. In fact, you can define your own desires and codify your startup's as a means to inspire and galvanize your organization.

Also, build the scoreboard—and make sure it's balanced. While I expect that you have goals for your organization, are they SMART? Cumulatively, do they align to the five dimensions we outlined in Chapter 6? Have departments drafted their own scorecards that correlate to the enterprise goals? While these ideally would be done before the start of a fiscal year, they can be done at almost any time without impeding the day-to-day. If anything, they help to focus efforts and help people prioritize. *Do not wait for next year. Or for the perfect moment. Get going.*

The precision of those targets and the tracking will depend almost entirely on the resources and history of your business. Businesses with many years of historical data and baselines to reflect upon are (theoretically) more likely to define accurate goals. Similarly, companies with analytics software and resources in place will have an easier time with performance measurement. For smaller or earlier stage businesses, the goal is not precision but rather practice. Set the SMART-est goals you can, based on whatever history and objectives you can point to, ensuring at the outset that the goals are, in fact measurable. If you cannot measure them, they are not worth prioritizing. It might be a goal, but by definition, it is not SMART.

Next, ask about problems. While the shift to problem-centricity is significant and hard-earned, you and your startup can begin by practicing the vernacular. "What problem are we solving?" "Why is that a problem?" "Is it a root problem?" "Is it a problem most worth solving?" By injecting this language and these questions into day-to-day meetings and conversations, you will be readying the team for the moment when you do lean out from solutions and tune in to problems.

If you are able to achieve the above, you have functionally begun to build the bridge from the status quo to your future GPS practice. Then as the next fiscal period approaches and your current road map of priorities is in process, you will be able to imagine how to get from "here" to "there." You can carve out the time, ahead of the new year, to consider and prioritize new goals and problems for the future, with an eye toward finalizing them before the next year begins.

Year one of GPS might be like building a footbridge—something you can all walk across but which you may still tread lightly on. The steps are all there. But perhaps the fidelity and rigor are not. Do not worry. Even in that first year, you will hear the benefits and the growth. By year two, you'll be ready to build a bridge you can drive across.

Start simple. Start at the start. Practice the practice. And eventually, you'll build that bridge.

Why GPS, One Last Time?

While implementing the practice is very important, the point of GPS is not simply the practice. *It's what the practice yields: healthy growth.* Growth that aligns to the founder's desires and to "The Why" of the startup. Growth that values evidence over ideas and curiosity over charisma. Growth that is more aligned and less susceptible to bias and hyperfunction. Through GPS, you'll be encouraging design thinking on an institutional level. You'll be continuously experimenting upon the problems most worth solving. You'll continually optimize the relationship between product and market. As importantly, your employees will know if their work is good, and why or why not.

Want proof? Here's what happened at Clearhead: Starting in our second year, when we shifted from a more traditionally Lean approach to the problem-centricity of GPS, we achieved four straight years of triple-digit growth. We sustained and actually expanded profit margins while reinvesting in growth. We were listed in the top 10 percent of the Inc. 5000 and voted one of Austin's "Best Places to Work." We had an uncanny employee retention rate in an extremely competitive labor market. Employees said they were happier. Clients kept asking for more Clearhead. And when my co-founders and I decided we wanted to sell the company, we did not even have to go to market. A few calls led to several offers. In short order, we exited with a better-than-market valuation.

My biggest regret with Clearhead is that I had not identified my own desires before we set GPS into motion. As a result, I paid the price of friction, as my startup's desires trumped my own. But now, several years removed, I can see the ways in which the practice did serve me, as a human, and the ways in which I desired things that the company could not serve. That realization has made me a better entrepreneur and, moreover, a more fulfilled entrepreneur. The work I do today, not the least of which includes writing this book, is all in accordance with my core desires. As a result, I grow how I hope to grow, not how my startup needs me to grow.

Most entrepreneurs and most businesses cannot say the same. They are likely operating with a mishmash of processes, or no process at all. Data is available but misused. Experiments are conducted but not understood. Goals are half-stated. Problems are considered either nuisances or emergencies. It all leads to the same destination: chaos, misalignment, employee malaise, employee migration, lack of learning, and ultimately, unhealthy growth or regression. This is what the startup world has become, and sorry to sound a little like a late-night infomercial, but there is a better way.

GPS is that better way.

chapter 12

GPS for Life

GPS is a practice originally designed for startups that ultimately works just as well for any institution hoping to achieve healthy growth. But GPS has potential beyond these organizations. It can be a tool for change and inclusion. It can also be a lens that is pointed inward, toward the entrepreneur themself. In this way, GPS is personal for me, as much as it is professional. It took me a quarter-century to get there, but after I left Clearhead I asked myself the same questions that GPS demands of a startup. It was only then that I got stuck on goals, wondering where they came from, and discovered my core desires.

Without GPS, I likely would have jumped back into founder mode, sprinting—hyperfunctioning—on my way to startup number four. Because of GPS, I realized that being the CEO of a startup never fulfilled me. And because of GPS, I've never felt more fulfilled than I do now. I balance my time between writing, serving other founders, serving other causes, listening, and seeing my family much, much more.

The last few years of my life have been, far and away, the happiest ones. And that is because I have employed GPS as something of a mantra. Along the way, I've been reminded that GPS is first and foremost a practice for business: it has limitations in the personal realm. On the other hand, it has practical applications beyond institutional and entrepreneurial growth.

GPS for Diversity

Because it engenders listening, GPS provides benefits that are especially relevant to the fractionalized and hyper-mediated times we live in today. In hindsight, the years 2012 through 2017—the highest growth years for Clearhead—seem almost quaint compared to the years that followed. On the other hand, those were also the years in which the Black Lives Matter movement and the seeds of #MeToo were coalescing. It's no coincidence, then, that this was also the window during which we confronted the challenge that I perhaps felt least equipped to confront—diversity in the workplace.

Though I consider myself to be empathetic, open-minded, and progressive, I am also a straight, middle-aged white guy who was, for most of his career, "the boss." It's through that lens and position that, in 2014 and 2015, I was struggling to respond to suggestions from our team that Clearhead was not sufficiently diverse.

By any reasonable measure, those suggestions were true. But my first response to the rumblings was defensiveness. If you'll recall from way back in Chapter 3, I'd previously stumbled when I was presented with the suggestion of bias in our interview methods and compensation policy. But here, the evidence was plain: Clearhead was about two-thirds male. We were over 80 percent Caucasian. And yet, I knew that those figures were all too common for American tech-focused startups. Also, I understood that the problem started further upstream, well before hiring decisions. Our applicant pool was similarly skewed—a disproportionate share of the resumes that came to us were from white men. Privately, I thought,

We are doing our best. I'm trying to do the right things! But I knew this was the wrong response.

My second reaction was the feeling of being overwhelmed. "I have to grow this company, keep our customers, employees, and shareholders happy, be a husband and father, *and* solve this?!" It didn't seem fair. I felt accused and ill-suited for the challenge. I was not a sociologist, an economist, or a lawyer. I didn't know how to solve the problem of diversity. In fact, I wasn't even sure that I knew what the problem was exactly. I wanted others to help diagnose the problem and prescribe the solution.

And so I assembled a group of Clearhead-ers who had been most vocal on the subject of D.E.I.A. (Diversity, Equity, Inclusion, Accessibility) and told them that this seemed too big and too complicated for one person to resolve. Then, I listened.

The group talked about diversity from the perspectives of race, gender, and class. They talked about how extroverts at the company were implicitly rewarded in ways that introverts were not. They talked about where and how we recruited applicants and what our interview process was like. They talked about the risks and rewards of quotas and the many ways we could define "diversity" and "equity." I listened and listened and got more and more overwhelmed. Until, finally, somebody said something that cut through it all for me. After a couple of hours, one Clearhead-er said something like, "Matty—ultimately, I don't think that the most important voices at Clearhead are being heard."

That revelation shook me. I knew it was probably true. I knew that the most valuable voices were not always making it into "the building" and that, when they did, they were not always being heard. This was a big problem. This would affect our growth. This was bad for business. All of which meant this was one of our problems most worth solving.

To change this, we went back to the beginning. In our company's mission and values, we stressed curiosity and empathy. But we also wanted to grow and succeed confidently. The only way to achieve all of those things was to ensure that the best voices were making it into the company and that they were being heard. Healthy, outsized growth does not come through homogeneity or the status quo. It progresses through difference and change. I was certain of that. I did not need to be a sociologist, an economist, or an iconoclast. I simply needed to reframe the challenge through GPS.

What did we desire? Confident growth, empathy, and curiosity. What were our goals concerning employee happiness and retention? What problems stood in the way of those goals and desires? There was a long list, but the short answer was that the most valuable voices were not always getting into the company, and when they were, they were not being heard. What were our solution hypotheses? There were many. Moreover, they were not simply mine to enact as policy. As with all things GPS, they were experiments that we would test and learn from.

In time, through problems, hypotheses, and experiments, our recruitment channels changed, our interview process changed, and our meeting agendas and formats changed. Within months, our applicant pool shifted. Soon thereafter, our employee census was more gender equitable. Our company was more colorful. I heard new approaches to problem solving that I, personally, never would have considered. It was not as though we fully solved the problem—that would not be a SMART goal. But we grew in correlation to our work on that problem.

Since my time at Clearhead, the push for D.E.I.A. has become louder and prouder. It has come up as a challenge for nearly every founder I've spoken to and for every board I've served on. And to those who've solicited my perspective, I've reminded them that—of course—D.E.I.A. is a sociological problem and an economic problem. But it is also a business problem. And to the extent that founders or board members are interested in growth, diversity is essential.

Diversity in the voices that make it into the building, diversity in the voices that speak, and diversity in the voices that are heard.

Personal Preferences

GPS allowed me to lean back, listen, and create a fairer, more representative workplace. And as you know by now, its benefits didn't end once I left Clearhead. After decades of chasing and reacting, *GPS helped me uncover my desires and be intentional, honest, and shame-free about what I choose to pursue in life.* These changes have been so drastic that I wonder now how I even survived before. As an entrepreneur, your startup is your child. I was incredibly unhealthy, but I pushed through, like a parent forever caring for their infant in their first few months. When stuck in that mode of thinking, care and growth are all that you know. It's all that you think about. Everything else is secondary. You do whatever it takes and then wake up after years of no sleep and wonder, how am I still alive?

And like parenthood, you eventually realize that more vigilance and less self-care absolutely do not equate to healthier child development. At some point, you have to nourish yourself. You have to dignify your own desires. If not, you'll collapse. And that is terrible for you and the child. As with child rearing, healthy startup growth requires the un-repression of desire.

Adapting GPS practices to your life can therefore be transformative. *GPS centers many of the important questions we often fail to ask ourselves*—what do I most desire, how will I know if I am successful, what problems are standing in the way of that success, what hypotheses do I have for resolving those problems? It's a means for keeping ourselves honest and holding ourselves accountable. It requires us to ask ourselves what we think we know, what we actually know, and why we are doing what we are doing. And through that asking and answering, we lead ourselves toward healthy growth.

But here's the rub: there's a big difference between the methods we use in our businesses and how we conduct our personal relationships. Being a founder of a startup affords a certain degree of authority. Independently and intrinsically, we have a high degree of control as to how we employ and care for our bodies and our minds. *But outside of work, in our day-to-day relationships with others, everything is different.* We are not employers, and the people in our lives are not our employees. Life is not transactional, and our value in our relationships will not be measured by ARR or EBITDA, market cap, or net worth.

For startups, GPS truly is an all-encompassing practice that elicits healthy growth. Personally, it can also be a useful—even necessary—diagnostic to help entrepreneurs check in and ensure that their lives are sufficiently aligned to their own desires and those of their startup. But it mostly stops there. Your life partners, your friends, and your children are in no way obligated to abide by GPS. You have no control over the matter. Trust me, when your spouse tells you that she's really upset with a friend or family member, "What problem are we trying to solve here?" is not the question you want to ask. Similarly, I can recognize the eye rolls of friends when I suggest that their argument sounds like a hypothesis. Though the spirit of GPS surely translates to nonbusiness life, the language and the practice have their limitations.

So I'm not recommending GPS as a "cure-all" or for interpersonal relationships, but that doesn't mean it won't have a significant impact in your life. You can use it to get closer to your fuller, truer self. You can use it to help set goals for yourself. You can use it to identify the problems you want to solve. And you can use it to articulate hypotheses and test solutions to the extent that those problems are intrinsic to you or specific to you.

GPS as the Alternative

As I mentioned all the way back in Chapter 1, while I was writing this book, there were a number of limited series on streaming services about the founders of WeWork, Theranos, and Uber. The subtext of each of these programs was functionally the same: these founders, while likely brilliant, are also deeply stunted (or worse). And there must be an inverse relationship between professional growth and personal development.

In these stories, according to the founders, more and faster is always better. Millions are never enough. Billions are just the beginning. For these entrepreneurs, the true desires are opaque and the problems are ignored. There are only solutions. There is only growth. And while I am happy that we have ride-sharing, and while I really enjoy working in WeWork spaces, I am completely unnerved by the prevailing narratives. The healthiest growth, in my experience, is not maximum growth. In fact, I've found that maximum growth leads to "terminal growth"—growth that threatens the core desires of the business and the entrepreneur. But also, I do not accept that entrepreneurial growth and institutional growth are inversely related.

I hope that, for those who are interested in these stories—whether they are entrepreneurs, employees of startups, or simply consumers of information about startup culture—GPS presents the *other* path. It's not the path that leads to spectacular implosions nor does it presume slow growth, "lifestyle" businesses. It's the one that grows iteratively in correlation to a set of personal desires rather than the desires of any prevailing narrative. *It's the antidote to the "uber-founder" (pun intended)* and the story we keep telling ourselves about the entrepreneur as antihero.

We need GPS in entrepreneurship now—not just to counter the impulses of our antiheroes and to empower "healthier" leaders—but to offset the worst potential of the technology we are constantly developing. We are more dependent upon and vulnerable to the power of algorithms and machine learning than ever before. This trend will continue. There's no way to reverse it: it's a technological imperative. And to be clear, it is not necessarily bad. It accelerates learning, discoveries, and conveniences that can make the world better. On the other hand, it also leads to fractionalization, echo chambers, and confirmation biases. We can see and hear only the information we "like," and artificial intelligences can superserve those likes.

Similarly, the "metaverse" is both inevitable and already all around us. And along with the prevalence of algorithms and artificial intelligence, real lives can increasingly feel like "derivative lives" consisting of avatars, handles, profile photos, and exclusively digital communication. I am not a futurist, but I am very far from a Luddite. I'm not suggesting that the inevitable is awful so much as I am saying that, without a path to healthy growth, more and faster will trump our core desires. Our physiology and psychology simply cannot match the speed of technology.

To the extent that entrepreneurship continues to be a job and startups continue to be composed of human beings, *we have the capacity to decide if we want to pursue growth that nourishes us or simply divides and then validates us.* Instead of assuming outcomes defined exclusively by speed, force, and volume, GPS considers the outcome in relation to desires, goals, and obstacles. In this way, GPS enables human resistance to dysmorphic startup growth and the unsustainable approach that many entrepreneurs take in pursuit of that image. GPS is like an inoculation—when practiced dutifully, it can keep us out of the echo chamber and reconnects us to intention.

Ultimately, like that inoculation, GPS is a solution for one entrepreneur, one startup. Then two entrepreneurs, two startups. Those one or two shots don't necessarily make a huge difference across a society. But do millions of people inoculating themselves with the power of listening make a difference? Probably.

conclusion

Back in the beginning, before the introduction to this book, before
the idea for this book, before we even had a name for it, the seeds of
GPS started with a simple question that my Clearhead co-founder,
Ryan, and I were asking ourselves: why do some designs work while
others fail? Next, we asked why certain products succeed while most
fail. How about startups themselves? How about the entrepreneurs
that founded those startups? The answers took us further back,
through the problems most worth solving that impacted the "smart-
est" goals that defined the extent to which our startup's desires were
fulfilled. It was almost always that simple: solve more problems than
you create, and you will observe growth. Solve the problems that
most correlate to your desires, and your growth will be healthy.

But then came the harder questions: How do I know what
problems are most worth solving? How do I know if my solution
is valid? How do I even know what my startup desires if I've never
asked what I most desire? We found the answers to these questions
through listening—pure and simple. Well, maybe not *that* simple.
We described listening as both a literal, auditory faculty as well as an
unbiased, good faith opening up to evidence and perspective.

And with that seemingly simple, probably romantic, metaphor,
we began our practice. We defined each step—how to listen and

what some pitfalls might be. Desires. Goals. Problems. Hypotheses. Experiments. Outcomes. Then we tried to put them all together into a continuous practice, acknowledging that there is no one best way to "do GPS." There are infinite ways, distinguished by degrees of fidelity and rigor.

Ultimately, GPS is really just an open source template. Like Linux, Python, Magento, and WordPress, it's designed to be what you make of it. Unlike those coding frameworks, though, GPS has firm constraints. And those constraints are what distinguish it from Lean Startup methodologies, which, to their credit, are more prescriptive in how evidence is employed and growth is achieved than Constraints theory. Put those two together though—Lean and Constraints—and account for desire, and you are ready for healthy growth: the sort of growth that provides lasting value for a startup while also enabling the founder to live a fulfilled life.

Just before finishing up my manuscript for this book, I participated in a GPS session for one of the startups I serve—an e-commerce agency. The founders had been growing steadily for a few years before we met, but they were so much more talented, ambitious, and capable than their results were indicating. They knew their product. They knew their market. They knew where they wanted to get to. But they needed some help getting there.

Our first year practicing GPS was, like all cold starts, hard work. We had to align on everything from the basic vocabulary and assumptions to desires, goals, and problems. We had to resist the urge to jump into solutions. And then we had to slowly, but confidently, propagate the practice out to other parts of the company. Twelve months later, this startup has grown by over 100 percent. Their net profit is far beyond their goals and the industry average. They've grown the staff considerably without losing a single employee. And they've sufficiently solved some of their problems most worth solving.

For this startup, everything about GPS was easier in year two. The desires were functionally the same. The founders were fluent in goal writing, and they came armed with some thoughts around problems for next year. What took many hours last year took less than an hour this year. What felt impossible thirteen months ago is practically a given now.

Both of these co-founders had newborn babies last year, and I was certainly worried for them. Would they burn out? Would startup growth come at the expense of their personal health? Or at the expense of their family? Obviously, only they know the answers to those questions. But based on what they shared and what I observed, their outsized growth certainly looks like healthy growth to me.

Whether you realize it or not, you've made your own investment in healthy growth as well. You picked up this book. You acknowledged that something was amiss with how we think about growth. You showed up and you stuck around and listened. Obviously, the next steps won't be easy. But they will be easier than the alternatives, including the status quo.

As you continue your practice, remember: there is no evidence that the wealthiest entrepreneurs are the happiest. Unicorns are not inherently better than workhorses. More is not necessarily better. While it might not require much for you to accept these claims, they go against the grain of prevailing discourse. In this book, I've asked you to look at growth differently—to not conflate it with "success." Success is almost always, insidiously, out of reach. It presumes something that does not exist: "the best."

Growth, on the other hand, is iterative. It's something to strive toward rather than to end at. Growth is something you can practice. So let's practice, practice, practice. Begin with an inventory of desires—for yourself, your company, your products, and so on. Start with those first poses and see how they feel. Then onto goals. And then problems. Lean out before you tune in.

Finally, I can only hope that, as you iterate and grow, you'll bring the spirit of experimentation to your practice. In other words, test and optimize GPS. While this book might serve as a blueprint for your practice, it will always, by definition, be a work in progress. GPS is less than ten years old. It's still a baby. Help it grow...healthy.

acknowledgments

I've been so lucky—I've founded companies with some of my dearest friends. But in all my life, I've only had one partner—and that is my wife, Megan. Megan has been by my side for two decades, three startups, one modest midlife crisis, hundreds of 4:00 a.m. departures and 1:00 a.m. arrivals, and thousands of inane complaints about work things that seemed really important to me at the time. Any good fortune that I've had, I owe to her. Most entrepreneurs leave the arena injured or worse. But Megan kept me intact and put me back together when I needed it most.

As for those co-founders, I would not have become an entrepreneur without my best friend, Christian Anthony, or my Insound co-founder, Ari Sass, who is perhaps the most generous person I have ever worked with. Sam Decker almost single-handedly created a universe of opportunity for me in Austin, while also teaching me everything I needed to know about startup culture. And finally, this book simply would not exist without my co-founder, Ryan Garner, whose insight into the "physics of growth" shaped the thesis statement for this book and for Clearhead. My time with Ryan included the highest highs, the hardest-earned victories, and the most respectful collaboration of my career.

Thank you to the many wonderful Clearheaders who helped test and optimize so many of the hypotheses contained in the pages that follow. Clearhead's very first designer, the wonderful Haley McMichael, provided all of the illustrations for this book. Thank you, Haley. The complete list of Clearheaders I could (and should) thank would be far too long to include here, but you know who you are.

Thank you to my favorite writers who are also, as it happens, accomplished "professional listeners." Since I was a teenager, I dreamed of one day being a music journalist (still dreaming). My love of writing was inspired initially by the likes of Robert Christgau and Greil Marcus and, in later years, Jessica Hopper, Chuck Klosterman, and Elizabeth Nelson. Their work has inspired me to write and listen more.

Finally, thank you to my parents, Susan and Barry Wishnow, and my brothers, Judd and Brandon. My whole life, they've always made me feel like I was capable of anything. They gave me the rarest of gifts: curiosity and confidence, with an extra dose of humility.

appendix

Helpful Books for A/B Testing and Optimization

- The Innovator's Hypothesis: How Cheap Experiments Are Worth More than Good Ideas by Michael Schrage
- A/B Testing: The Most Powerful Way to Turn Clicks Into Customers by Dan Siroker and Pete Koomen
- You Should Test That: Conversion Optimization for More Leads, Sales and Profit or The Art and Science of Optimized Marketing by Chris Goward
- Statistical Methods in Online A/B Testing: Statistics for Data-Driven Business Decisions and Risk Management in E-Commerce by Georgi Zdravkov Georgiev
- Experimentation Works: The Surprising Power of Business Experiments by Stefan H. Thomke

Helpful Books for Measurement and Analytics

- Web Analytics 2.0: The Art of Online Accountability and Science of Customer Centricity by Avinash Kaushik
- Lean Analytics: Use Data to Build a Better Startup Faster by Alistair Croll and Benjamin Yoskovitz
- Web Analytics Demystified by Eric Peterson
- The Balanced Scorecard: Translating Strategy into Action by Robert S. Kaplan and David P. Norton
- Information is Beautiful by David McCandless